I Woke Up
and
Chose Peace

I Woke Up *and* Chose Peace

Reclaiming Your SANITY, SERENITY, and SELF in a World That Won't Let You Rest

ASHLEY GREEN, LMSW

I WOKE UP AND CHOSE PEACE
Reclaiming Your Sanity, Serenity, and Self in a World That Won't Let You Rest

The information in this book is based on the author's knowledge, experience, and opinions. The ideas and methods described in this book are not intended to be a definitive set of instructions. You may discover other methods and materials to accomplish the same end result. Your results may differ.

To request permissions, please contact the publisher at:
Verde Press
chanaegreen11@gmail.com

Paperback ISBN: 979-8-218-61661-8
First Paperback Edition: July 2025
Edited by: Sabrina Butler, Unpolished Words
Cover by: Make Your Mark Publishing Solutions
Layout by: Make Your Mark Publishing Solutions

This book is dedicated to any person that has been missing peace. May you find all the peace and respect yourself enough to choose peace over chaos every time.

Contents

Author's Note

I was born and raised in good ole Macon, Georgia. The church leaders, educators, mentors I met in Macon, and my grandparents and parents are the reason I am who I am today. I will forever be grateful for Macon. Growing up in Macon taught me so many life lessons. The one lesson that will forever be close to my heart is just because you are not rich monetarily, does not mean you won't forever be rich with love from God and family. My family did not have much, but we had so much love for each other and God. And because of the love that was poured into me, I am able to pour so much love into the world.

Let me go ahead and put this out there, I'm a country girl. Throughout this book you'll see words such as "y'all," "good ole," and "yes ma'am." I've been taught proper grammar, but I want y'all to get to know me. Talking in my country girl voice gives y'all a feel for who I am. This is my first book, but it won't be my last. I have already started on my second one. I just need y'all to know who you're taking advice from. I love when I read books and I can relate to the person; it feels like I know them from somewhere. Well, some of you may know me and some may not. After reading this book, though, we are going to be friends or even play cousins. If you see me around town, don't hesitate to say, "Hey girl hey." I promise I'll speak back. I might even give you a big ole hug.

Introduction

Heyyyyyy there. I'm so glad you decided to purchase this book. I'm so proud of you. Purchasing this book was a great investment. Have you been in a space of chaos for way too long and unsure of how to kick it to the curb? Is your body craving a lighter feeling? Do you want to make the best out of your life? Are you allowing people to offer you less than what you deserve? Do you have peace sometimes but are unsure how to *remain* at peace? If you answered yes to any of those questions, then this book is for you, my friend. Come on in.

This book will help you learn how I gained my peace and why it is important for you to gain yours. My name is Ashley Green, LMSW. Social work was instilled in me at a young age. I just did not know then that it was called social work. I would see people in my community, church, and school always helping those who were in need and those acts would make my heart smile. Making a difference in the world brings me so much joy. There's nothing else I would rather be doing at this point in my life. And to think I considered becoming a schoolteacher and a lawyer. God said no ma'am no ma'am that is not the plan. When God gives you a plan, you cannot go against that plan. God needed me to do a job that only special individuals can do. If you work in the social work field, you understand why you must be special to work in this field. Being a social worker requires a lot of energy, empathy, compassion, resource seeking, patience, and time. As a social worker I have my hands in all sorts of things. One thing I love about the profession is how diverse it is and how many avenues there are.

Right now, my passion is medical social work. It is important that I can always do my job effectively, so that is one reason I am big on peace. For me to thrive in my personal and professional life, I must do all that I can to ensure that my peace is protected 99.99 percent of the time. You may be wondering what protecting your peace looks like. Peace is enjoying the simple things in life. Peace can be something as simple as using a lavender towel to help you cool down from your hike or run. Peace can be swinging your feet at the park with a good ole margarita in hand. And when you lose sight of that peace, your body will send off signals in the form of anxiety, pain, lethargy, hopelessness, and more.

I hope that you are comfortable in your favorite chair with your favorite drink and snack right now. Get ready to start your peaceful journey. I am so excited for you to gain all the peace you can. Peace is going to be at your front door peeping in like, "Heyyyyyyy." I'm going to help you learn to let it on in, and you can thank me later. Waking up and choosing peace was the best decision I've ever made. I not only woke up and chose peace for me, but I chose to always share my peace with the world when given the chance. "You shall not take vengeance or bear a grudge against your people." Love your neighbor as yourself: I am the Lord." (Leviticus 19:18) You better get in your bible if you're not already, because that's part of the journey of peace. I pray that after reading this book you wake up and choose peace for yourself and others. Let's keep the peace wave going friend.

In this book you will learn about peace and what it means. I'm going to share my story about gaining peace. I will share with you how science can be included in peace. Then, we're going to discuss how to maintain peace once you've got it. I will include personal stories and a plethora of options for you to try on your own. There will also be room for reflection on everything you've learned. You will then officially get started on your peace journey with some advice and a good ole word from the Lord. And who doesn't love resources? At the very end you'll find resources to keep the peace long after you read this book.

After reading this book, buy the next person their own copy and open that front door to peace for them as well. Don't be stingy now. I truly believe in the saying "sharing is caring." In this book I will be nothing but honest with you about my full journey, beginning to end. Before I begin, I do want to thank everyone that has helped me in my peace journey that I may not mention in this book for everything that you've poured into me. Your love and patience will never go unnoticed. I pray that you are at peace right now and continue to live a peaceful life. And I just want to thank everyone that is just now hopping on this journey with me for giving me a chance to pour into you and guide you. Now, take my hand and allow me to guide you on an amazing journey, friend.

Peace

A state of tranquility or quiet. Freedom from disquieting or oppressive thoughts or emotions.

"Peace can be found in many different ways. Peace is versatile."

—Ashley Green

"Never be in a hurry; do everything quietly and in a calm spirt. Do not lose your inner peace for anything whatsoever, even if the whole world seems upset."

—Saint Francis de Sales

"You can find peace amidst the storms that threaten you."

—Joseph B. Wirthlin

CHAPTER 1

Finding Peace

On a peaceful note ......

Peace is the simplest thing one can obtain. No matter what, "protect your peace." Protecting your peace may look different from your peers and that is just fine. Protect it like your life depends on it because it really does. Protect your peace because it feels good. Protect your peace because it makes you look good. Protect your peace because it's your peace and your peace is to be protected.

The first time I experienced peace was at the age of twenty-six. I started living for myself and stopped living for other people. We get so caught up in what other people are doing and we feel that we need to be doing some of those things as well. Someone else's journey will never be your journey. Let me repeat that, someone else's journey will never be your journey.

I started doing what truly made me happy regardless of what anyone thought. I have always been a confident person, but I knew I was not revealing all that God put inside of me. I started to maximize on my confidence. I started to really glow and grow. It was time to blossom. Holding back? I no longer knew what that was. I started to stand taller than I actually am. I started to speak up on important issues. I started to wear what I wanted and how I wanted. My peace beamed through any room I walked in. My peace started to rub off on anyone that sat next to me. Peace became so addictive, and I just had to get more and more of it.

I started to maximize on my confidence. I started to really glow and grow. It was time to blossom. Holding back? I no longer knew what that was. I started to stand taller than I actually am.

Living for myself was one of the best things I ever did for myself. After I started glowing and growing, I knew finding my peace was not done. Everyone has their own definition, but here is mine. Glowing is when you physically look happy. Your skin starts to pop and shine. Growing is internal. You find yourself learning from mistakes and evolving in all aspects of your life. You start developing new thinking patterns and opening endless opportunities for yourself. You find yourself wanting to be petty in a moment, but instead choosing peace over violence. It just feels so good. I woke up one day and chose peace.

Friendship

In order to grow, sometimes you have to leave some individuals behind. Some of my friendships were just toxic and not peaceful. I had friends that gave off too much negative energy. I was very close with "some of those friends" and wanted to hang on to them. But I had to ask myself, "Hang on for what girl?" When you meet people and you develop close-knit relationships over time, it is hard to just cut them off one day. You had all the fun in the world with them, told them your darkest secrets, and cried on their shoulders at times. But just because you experience all of that with a person over a period does not mean they were placed in your life to be there forever. Letting go of those relationships was a hard process for me, and I promise you it did not take place in a day. If you just looked away from this book for a second to check your phone because this idea made you uncomfortable, you need to know: Everyone is not meant to be in your life for forever. God will replace those friends—and with peaceful ones at that. Just sit all the way back and watch. "Friends" will disturb your peace as long as you let them, trust me. And they will not give a damn. Let me repeat that. Friends will disturb your peace as long as you let them and not give a damn. Excuse my French, but I had to say it that way to put some emphasis on it. I'm dancing and emphasizing. (If you've watched the show *The Game*, you know what I'm talking about.)

There I was trying to be nice and give those people chance after chance. God had to reveal things to me the hardest way since I was not trying to make a move and let them go myself. Those individuals and what they stood for really came to the light. There I was, watching from my imaginary backseat, disappointed that I was still hanging on. Some of those friends were saying hateful things, throwing shade they thought I didn't catch, and had me doing things I knew were not right, lying to the ones I love. There was one friend that had this mentality that everyone was out to get her. That was my girl too. I couldn't say or do just about anything around her without having to think really deeply about it. We fell out at least three times. I should have let it go after the first time huh? But again, it is hard sometimes. After I realized my worth and how important my peace was, I cut those individuals off one by one. There was another friend that had an issue with everything I did. As long as I wasn't doing better than her, we were good. When I started talking about goals I had for myself, she questioned it all. She asked me questions that had me wondering if I should even go after any of the goals. She clearly didn't want to see me win. As that heavy weight started to drop, more peace entered.

I narrowed my friend list down to about six friends—the best six friends a girl could ask for. I no longer felt like I had to have a bunch of friends to be worthy or popular. Who really has the time for twenty friends anyway? I started doing more in life, such as obtaining degrees, being a great aunt, working, and just living my best life. That was taking up majority of my time anyway. I no longer had time for toxicity. I bet God was asking throughout the process "My child, my child, when will thou listen?" And for those of you who do have twenty friends, are they quality relationships? I ask that question because we are all so busy dealing with adult things. I don't even get to talk to the friends I do have every day, every week, or month. How does one have time to pour into twenty friends? Please let your girl know.

Eliminating friendships that aren't peaceful or purposeful is worth considering. Do you have a friend or friends that you are constantly trying to work with to see if things will get better? Questioning whether they have your back or not? Are they supportive? Are they understanding? A lot of the people who I put in the category of friends should have been associates instead. But this is where I had to live and learn. It is ok to not consider everyone a friend. Compartmentalizing is a thing for a reason. Now I'm not saying go out there and cut your homegirl or homeboy of twenty years off after one disagreement. But do take some time and consider: Is the relationship solid?

> Eliminating friendships that aren't peaceful or purposeful is worth considering.

Love

I'm sure we all have been in a relationship that was just too hard to let go of, right? Raise your hand if that has been you. You're in safe space, I promise. Go ahead, raise that hand and say it out loud. I promise I will not judge you. Don't beat yourself up too much; just please learn and never ever do it again. Your time is precious. I was in a relationship with someone who I thought I was going to be with for forever. I just knew we were going to get married and have some beautiful chocolate babies. We had names picked out, Godparents, and the whole nine yards. When I met him, I thought he was the finest thing on the planet. He was fine, but not worth all the drama. We were together for three years and some change, but it should have been three months and some change to be honest. We had our ups and too many downs. I prayed and prayed to God that he would work things out for us. And again, he said no ma'am no ma'am.

The signs were all there. We broke up so many times, and my friends and family were over it. I loved him with everything in me. We had many similar life goals and we motivated each other through college. Yes, we met in college, and I thought we were going to be able to tell the world, "He/she is my college sweetheart." Maybe helping each other through college was the reason we were together for so long. Remember, God sometimes places people in your life for a season to help accomplish a certain goal and that is all. Once the goal is reached, God expects us to move forward. But of course, we have to be disobedient at times. There were so many red flags, and of course I chose to ignore them each and every time. I remember being in history class and not being able to focus because we broke up for maybe the fourth time at that point. I was in class calling one of my best friends at that time to reach out to him for me. She had known him before I did, so I thought maybe she could talk some sense into him. Thinking about that now just makes me disappointed in myself. Why did I want my friend to talk some sense into someone that so-called loved me? I remember the pages in my history book were drenched from crying so hard. Whew!

We were in college, so he was young and immature. He went out one night with a few of his friends. During this time, we were not together but still on speaking terms. We were on a break because he claimed he "didn't know what he wanted." He and his friends were out partying and got pulled over with open beer bottles in the car. You probably already know where I'm going with this. He got arrested because it was his car. And guess who he called? Me of course. He begged and pleaded his case as to why I should help him. I was in the bed minding my single business. I remember calling my daddy freaking out because I did not know what to do. I had never experienced anything like that in my life. Me being the nice person I was, I bailed him out with the little money I had left over from my Walgreens check. And to put the icing on the cake, later that week he asked me to be his girlfriend again because he said, "I had been there for him no matter what." Why did I allow someone's son to play in my face like that? That version of me clearly did not know my worth. If I had known my true worth, after the second break up I would have headed for the hills. Head for the hills, please, after the second time.

Now I can look back and laugh at how crazy those years were. I was so not protecting my peace. I wasn't even thinking about protecting my peace either. I didn't even know what peace was. When things finally ended, I was in a funk for almost an entire summer. But when I was out of the funk, there was peace saying, "Hey girlfriend." I was glowing and just so darn happy. We don't realize why God does certain things until after the storm passes all the way. I was so happy that I let that situation go. I no longer felt obligated to help make someone else's son happy for a while. I found out so much about myself and I was in the streets all summer. I was in the streets while I was in the funk, but I was *really* in the streets after the funk had passed.

The streets were in Atlanta, Georgia, enjoying brunch, day

7

parties, lounges, night parties, and relaxing by the pool with my bestie Ronda and some other friends. My friends and my family poured all the love into me. I remember one day just riding down Clairmont Road in Atlanta listening to Moneybagg Yo and just jamming. I smiled from ear to ear because I was at peace. I just really want to thank my best friend Ronda for that summer. Ronda not only made sure I was having fun, but she lifted me up. She helped me see my worth and that it was not the end of the world. Ronda and I have been best friends for over thirteen years. Get you a few Ronda's and call it a day. Thank you, sunshine. When I say God does things for a reason, I mean it. I really need to redo that summer at some point in the future. That summer was everything my soul needed and more. During times like those it's best to have people that you can lean on to help you build yourself back up and realize that you are the prize and nothing less. It seems like it is the end of the world in the midst of a breakup, but there is something on the other side of that breakup that is better. The sun shines and your heart is smiling.

Career

Where was I going in my career? I graduated undergraduate with my bachelor's in psychology. It was a very rewarding degree and challenging at times. Psychology was one of the next best things to a degree in Education, in my opinion. Learning about the human brain and what chemical imbalances could do to an individual was interesting. During one of my classes, we learned about patients with schizophrenia. My professor put on audio for us to hear what some patients that are diagnosed with it hear every day if not treated. After hearing the voices and how distracting they were, I knew I had made the right decision in changing majors from Early Childhood

Education. I was sold and ready to learn more. Not only was it an interesting degree, I made some amazing connections. I have great relationships with two professors from that time, and to this day I can text and call them when needed.

But to be honest, it was hard getting a job with just a psychology degree. The reason I got the job I did as fast as I did was because my school took us to Atlanta to a job fair a few months before I graduated. There were so many jobs present at this fair. I was walking around looking at all the tables and I was losing faith. None of the jobs called out to me in the slightest way. Then I rolled up on a table that said, "ABA therapy with children." Now we were getting somewhere. The employer locked eyes with me and called me right on over. There I was rushing right on over too.

We talked for about thirty minutes. She gave a nice presentation and explained it all so well. I was sold on ABA therapy. I knew I wanted to make a difference and work with children, so it was the perfect starter job. Just because you start somewhere doesn't mean that's where you will end. Please remember that. I figured I could also use some of the techniques I learned in my child and adolescent class. The employer gave me her information and we stayed in contact leading up to right before graduation. Guess who had a job shortly after graduation?

I worked with children who had autism for a year and a half. It had its ups and downs. I might have gotten hit by a few tables and chairs along the way, but it paid the bills and it was rewarding as well. As I was working one day, I realized that I was not revealing everything that was in me. I thought about the work I was doing and what I wanted to do in the future. A light bulb went off that day. I'd had a conversation with my advisor from undergrad, Ms. Stavely, years before. We were talking about future plans and what I could do in the future. I remember us talking about my personality. She said I had the personality to become a social worker. I did not know what a social worker was at the time and nor was I interested in learning what one was. The only thing that was on my mind at that time was finishing my last year of school with decent grades.

During that moment when the light bulb went off, I thought about that conversation, I decided to research social work and what it entailed. One of the best things I read in my search was "helps oppressed individuals thrive." I screamed on the inside. That brought me peace. That's what I wanted to do. "I want to help make the world a better place." "I have the heart for this." Those are just a few things I said to myself. In that moment, I found my purpose. (Thank you so much Ms. Stavely for that amazing conversation.)

Now that my purpose was found, I had to do something about it. My fingers went to clicking on my keyboard in search of social work programs. It was between Georgia State University and Kennesaw State University. Georgia State is a great school for any degree, but my anxiety was so bad then, and there was no way I was walking all over downtown Atlanta to get to where I needed to go.

Choosing Kennesaw was one of the best decisions I have ever made. Kennesaw's program taught me an ample amount of information about social work. The director of the program was amazing! Dr. Irene McClatchy was one hell of a woman. She made social work seem so effortless and worth the ride that was ahead. She gave me a tour of the social work department, discussed what would be expected of me, and welcomed me with open arms. She already knew I was going to choose the program the day I left the tour.

My graduate experience was amazing from beginning to end. The program prepared me to be one of the best social workers in Georgia. I pray for that same experience if you are considering graduate school or school in general. When God speaks, remember to listen to him. He shall not steer you in the wrong direction. I'm at peace with my career choice. I'm always brainstorming projects that will help my community here in Atlanta and back home in Macon, GA. I don't believe in just going to work and offering my services there. I want to make a difference all over the world y'all. And I actually make the time to stay up to date on the latest social work practices to ensure that I am offering the world the most current and best information. Most of the jobs that I've had in the past were jobs that just kept the lights on with no real purpose behind them. It warms my heart knowing that I did something, whether small or big, to contribute to someone else's success. I love waking up in the morning and getting ready to head to work. Now, that is peace. Heading to work, jamming to some of my favorite tunes or listening to a podcast knowing that I'm actually going to do what is purposeful to me.

> Now that is what you call peace. When you can find your purpose and still find time to explore other activities that you enjoy, do it.

Do you think I'm going to stop at "just" being a social worker? Absolutely not! I'll be that social worker that wrote this book and started businesses, organizations, and more. Now that is what you call peace. When you can find your purpose and still find time to explore other activities that you enjoy, do it. I'm a social worker first before anything else. I've also been blessed with the gift of creativity. Interior design has become a passion of mine in the recent years. I've taken a course to perfect my skills, read books, and more. The world has taught me if you are given a gift, you should act on it. The worst thing that can happen is you don't like the career as much as you thought you would. And if that happens, you pick yourself up and explore another gift you have until you find the one that is the most fulfilling.

It took me breaking up with friends, finding the career that was for me, and leaving the guy I thought was going to be my husband to find peace. Finding your peace will look different from how I found mine and that is perfectly fine. Let this chapter simply be a guide to your pen when you sit down today or soon and make that list.

Reflection Questions: Is this friend or significant other really for me? Do I love my career or is it just keeping the lights on? What is my true purpose? What does peace mean to me? Do I really want a peaceful life?

"Do not let the behavior of others destroy your inner peace."

—*Dalai Lama*

CHAPTER 2

Peace Theory

On a peaceful note......

Peace is deep inside. Peace is science. Peace is taught. Peace is therapy. Peace is intentional. Peace is open-minded. Peace is simple.

I f this is supposed to be a guide, then including research is necessary. It is one thing to take my word on inner peace and how to gain it, but to read research on exactly what inner peace is and feels like is another. Also, reading research on ways you can achieve personal peace and learning ways to help achieve peace for our communities is noble.

As a social worker, it is my duty to promote and encourage the well-being of people and communities. And in doing that, it is important that I share the education that was so expensive with you. Grad school took your girl through it. It was only two years but felt like five. I had to write papers that were twenty-two pages long at times. That was some trauma, but I wouldn't trade it for anything in the world. I always remind myself of the phrase "sharing is caring." So here we go, friend. It is imperative that I explain the connection of social work and peace. When I break it all down you will understand that gaining peace can be so simple. I will give you a glimpse of what social workers do and how we can help promote peace in the world. Take advantage of this information and take plenty of notes. Just call me Dr. Green in this chapter. Dr. Green has a nice ring to it. This chapter may just inspire your girl to go back to school to get a PhD. Over the past few years, I have flirted a lot with the idea, so we shall see. I hope you have your spiral notebook and number two pencil handy. Here we gooooooo.

There has been little research attention paid to inner peace, a fundamentally balanced mental state that has been sought after throughout human history (Delle Fave et al., 2016). I had to insert that because people before our times were trying to gain peace. They just needed a book like this one to help them guide them to peace. Searching for articles was not an easy task because most of them tend not to focus on inner peace but more on the term well-being.

Inner peace and "well-being" run in the same circle. You might as well call them cousins. They are very similar, but with a minor difference. Well-being focuses on a person's happiness, health, and comfortability. But inner peace? There is a metaphor that has often been used to describe inner peace: The inner world of the mind is like a calm, quiet, and clear lake (Phillippe, 2002). It is a quiet that does not imply eventless or emptiness of inner experiences. But it does imply a different mode of inner experience which is always clear, gentle, and grounded no matter the nature of the outer event it is associated with (Lee, 2021). Basically, true inner peace is when that fool on the highway cuts you off causing you to swerve just a little, but you have a calmness over you that prevents you from reacting in a foolish way. You don't go flying down I-75 like a NASCAR racer trying to catch up to them and curse them out. You just continue driving and jamming to that song you're listening to. You have trained yourself to be calm and grounded inside no matter what happens on the outside because that feels good to you. That is your center; stick beside it.

There are many things in life that will challenge us to be and do something out of our normal routine.

> There are many things in life that will challenge us to be and do something out of our normal routine. DON'T FALL FOR IT! Just imagine if you allowed negativity to get you all worked up every time it came knocking on your door. You would be one tense and stressed individual.

DON'T FALL FOR IT! Just imagine if you allowed negativity to get you all worked up every time it came knocking on your door. You would be one tense and stressed individual. You would have wrinkles before your time from all that balling your face up. If you are intentional about practicing peace, you will forever live a life of peace. Just repeat and dance to the next lines.

I am peace and peace is me.
I am peace and peace is me.
I am peace and peace is me.

Whew! Didn't that feel good? Try singing that song when you are faced with challenges in life. *Everything does not deserve your reaction.* Remember, your energy is sacred and what you allow to steal your peaceful energy one time will probably do it again and again. Just as a quiet lake clearly mirrors clouds, birds, and other happenings passing over it, people with deep inner peace experience their life happenings with great clarity. Great clarity = inner peace. So basically, *no matter what* flies over your life and comes your way, you have trained yourself deeply to find peace in that moment. Please write that down on your bathroom mirrors, sticky notes, and all places you look at often.

Now after you do that, please hold on tight, because the rest of this chapter is very thought provoking. After reading it, I hope and pray you think about everything you read carefully and thoroughly to obtain the best results not only for yourself but for people around you that could also use peace in their lives. Now before you say something like "Hold on, I thought I was just reading this book to get guidance on how I can gain and obtain peace for *me*, but now I have to share it with others and help them as well?" Sharing is caring, friend. I mentioned that earlier, remember? You'll thank me later. If your grandmother is anything like mine was, she would want you to share and help others gain peace. "That's the Christian thing to do," she would say. Now have an open mind and heart when reading the rest of this chapter. And remember class is in session, so no interruptions.

Now what you are about to read discusses ways and concepts that will help you gain and remain at peace individually and in your community. When I was a therapist, I had clients that were dealing with various issues. Many of my clients were in therapy for things such as sexual assault, low self-esteem, parenting issues, diagnosed mental disorders, and more.

Social work theories are frameworks that help guide our practices and understand the behavior of individuals. Theories help us help clients, aka peace seekers exchange unwanted behaviors for better behaviors, cope with life stressors, and change their narrative, just to name a few results. Working as a therapist gave me a different appreciation for theories because I got a chance to see them help so many clients each session. Those clients no longer exhibited the unhealthy behaviors that caused them and their loved ones stress. Who wants to continue living a life with behaviors they know are wrong or that people are constantly bringing up to them? NO ONE! Who wants to continue allowing their past to hold them back? I hope not you. It's your time to reclaim your sanity, serenity, and self in a world that won't let you rest.

Long after I left therapy, I was able to use the theories in the hospital setting and in my personal life. There are a plethora of theories including some I have yet to use. The main theories that I did use in sessions were Cognitive Behavioral Theory (CBT), Empowerment Theory, Solution Focused Theory, Resilience Theory, and Narrative Theory. We won't discuss each of them, but I hope to teach you a bit to get you started and motivated to go to therapy if you have already been thinking about it. Or if you're not ready to go to therapy, you can practice them on your own. If you're still wondering what social work theories has to do with you and gaining peace, well just sit tight and buckle up. Let's get into it.

Cognitive Behavioral Therapy

This is a guide, so I had to bring everything that I could out of my toolbox to help you. I find myself using this first theory a lot in my daily life. I am human just like you, friend. Self-maintenance = peace. CBT and I have become best friends at this point. At the end of this book, I want you to be able to say, "She laid it all out for me and now I just have to get to work."

CBT is a form of psychological treatment that has been demonstrated to be effective for a range of problems including depression, anxiety disorders, alcohol and drug use disorders, marital problems, eating disorders, and severe mental illness. Cognitive behavioral therapy was put into place to help one create better thinking patterns. The idea behind CBT is that if you can change the way you think, you can change the way you feel (Ray J Thomlison & Barbara Thomlison, 2017, p. 55). Changing those constant negative thoughts into positive ones will help increase peace in your life.

Just imagine dealing with a mental disorder such as anxiety and you are constantly having anxious thoughts that are preventing you from landing the dream job you desire. You really want to step out and take some risk. You keep having thoughts like "What if I fail?" "What if no one likes what I'm offering?" and "I don't know where or how to start." Those thinking patterns will forever hold you back and that is just not peace. I want better for you, and I know you do too. Those thoughts are taking over and you have been letting them win the battle each and every time. Stop it today. Pretty please! Instead of those thoughts,

> Those thinking patterns will forever hold you back and that is just not peace. I want better for you, and I know you do too.

turn them around and say things such as, "The world will like what I'm doing, and if they don't, I will still push forward," or "I will win because I don't have a reason not to win."

Changing your thinking patterns doesn't happen overnight. It takes practice and you must be intentional about it. Let me repeat that. YOU HAVE TO BE INTENTIONAL ABOUT CHANGING YOUR THOUGHTS. I'm done screaming at you friend (for now), but I really need you to understand that. This is why therapy is very important to consider, because if you are having severe anxiety about advancing in one part of your life, then you are probably also having it in other areas of your life as well. A therapist can help you work through whatever it is causing you stress. I'm going to bring you along on a therapy session. I bet you didn't think you would be attending therapy in this book, but I'm trying to keep you on your toes. (I've got some more good stuff in the latter part of this book just waiting on you.) This therapy session demonstrates how a session with me would look from beginning to end.

Dr. Green: Hello, my name is Ashley and it is so nice to meet you. What brings you in today?

Peace Seeker: I am having severe anxiety and I can't seem to land the dream job I desire.

Dr. Green: You are having severe anxious thoughts, and they are keeping you from getting your dream job. Is that what I heard you say?

Peace Seeker: Yes. That is 100% correct. And I want that to change because I am just tired of being stuck in life, frustrated, and left behind. My peers are just passing me by and I feel like a loser.

Dr. Green: I can sense from your body movements, your tone, and word choice that you are frustrated and tired. Let's start off light today, since this is your first session. I like to build rapport with my clients before diving too deep. What do you do for a living? What are some favorite hobbies? What do your family dynamics look like?

[*I like to build rapport with clients by asking them these kinds of questions. This lets them speak freely and shows them that they matter, and that we are partners in sessions. And toward the end of the first session, we can discuss the issue at hand very lightly.*]

Dr. Green: How long has your anxiety been in your life?

Peace Seeker: Been in my life? What does that mean?

Dr. Green: Well, I reference the anxiety as being in your life because it has become a part of you. When you speak about yourself, do you say things like, "My anxiety won't let me do that; I have to stop"?

Peace Seeker: Yes, I do actually. It has always been attached to me.

Dr. Green: Well during our sessions let's focus on detaching from the anxiety, and instead of it being in you, we are going to externalize it. We are going to change our thought process about the anxiety as well by implementing goals. So, hold on tight; we have a lot of work ahead. Do you think you can commit to coming to therapy once a week or every other week?

Peace Seeker: I can most definitely commit to once a week.

Dr. Green: Great to hear. After each session I will assign you homework. We will do work in our sessions, but you also have to practice at home to get better and reach your desired goals. Let's do a small exercise today. Write down "What if I fail?" at the top of my whiteboard. Under it write out scenarios that could take place if you fail.

Peace Seeker: Okay, I'm done.

Dr. Green: That is a long list of scenarios! Can you read off one of the scenarios for me please.

Peace Seeker: If I fail I will be laughed at and embarrassed.

Dr. Green: If you fail you will be laughed at and embarrassed. No one likes to be laughed at or embarrassed, for sure. I was laughed at when I mispronounced a word one time. It was embarrassing because I should have known how to say that word. We were not made to be perfect individuals though. We all make mistakes at times, and that is alright. That is what I took from that situation.

Peace Seeker: You're so right about that.

Dr. Green: Well, we will stop there on that assignment. For your homework, I want you to take that list you just wrote and break down every scenario you wrote. Next session, we will discuss each one and attempt to turn them into positive stories over time. But before we end today's session, I do want to go over my expectations and rules in my office and goals for yourself.

After going to therapy for a while this client learned how to manage their anxiety better and were able to take plenty of risk. By the end of the sessions, they no longer thought about the consequences of failing or what others thought. The client was turning negatives into positives left and right. CBT takes practice and willingness. The client utilized the list he made of consequences if he fails to challenge his negative thoughts. He replaced his negative thoughts with more realistic ones. He monitored over time how new behaviors and thinking patterns made him feel. As I mentioned to the client above, try externalizing your anxiety instead of continuing to allow it to live rent free in your mind. Grab a stuffed animal and pretend it is your anxiety. This may sound weird, but it was such a great exercise that I learned in grad school. Sit that bear in front of you, preferably. The bear's name is Anxiety. Tell anxiety what he or she has caused you in life thus far. Let Anxiety know that they are not the boss of you. You are the boss of them. Don't continue letting anxiety be a part of you like my client above to the point where it is holding you back from your talents. Utilize the CBT method to evict anxiety. Anxiety is living rent free and if you are living in the same United States of America that I am living in, things (like rent) are too high for something to be living off of you for free. After several months worth of therapy sessions, you should have a great concept of CBT and how to use it to your advantage. Remember CBT = peace. That was an example of how CBT can be used to change negative thinking into positive thinking. I also wanted to give you a feel of how an initial session

> Anxiety is living rent free and if you are living in the same United States of America that I am living in, things (like rent) are too high for something to be living off of you for free.

should feel like. There are plenty of CBT workbooks that you can order online to explore on your own if you are not ready yet to seek the help of a professional. There will be a list of those resources at the end of this book. (Social workers love giving out resources. So, it's only right.)

Try the exercise below with some negative thoughts you may be having. "Think about your reasoning behind the thought and break it all the way down. What is causing the thought? Why do I have the thought? Write down the negative thoughts and then turn it into a positive thought. Continue to practice all the time until it becomes second nature to you. The goal is to eventually be able to catch yourself when you start thinking negatively and turn it into a positive thought. Place this quote somewhere you look at often. "My thoughts will not get the best of me."

Negative thought:

_____

_____

_____

_____

_____

Replacement thought:

_____

_____

_____

_____

_____

Negative thought:

_____

_____

_____

_____

_____

_____

Replacement thought:

_____

_____

_____

_____

_____

_____

Negative thought:

_____

_____

_____

_____

_____

_____

_____

Replacement thought:

_____

_____

_____

_____

_____

_____

Empowerment Theory

Lee's empowerment approach deals with empowering people across the individual life span and in families, groups, and communities to develop their capabilities and assets and change noxious environments (Lee & Hudson, 2017). Empowerment is a reflexive activity, a process capable of being initiated and sustained only by those who seek power or self-determination. Others can only aid and abet in this empowerment process. The empowerment process resides in the person, not the helper (Lee & Hudson, 2017). When people are empowered, they feel like they can conquer the world. When you are empowered, you should feel free of fear. Goodbye fear and hello peace.

Let's step outside of our individual world for a minute and think about the communities we are from that may be in chaos and have never experienced anything close to calmness. If you and others from your community are in positions to empower your community to do great things that will bring about peace in the neighborhood, *do it*. At times, we sit with our loved ones and complain about the toxicity in the communities we grew up in or the ones that we currently live in. I see it too often in my community back home. I'm even guilty of doing it sometimes. Let's stop complaining and learn how to utilize Lee's approach to empower people instead of looking down on them. It is easy to look at and judge others based off of circumstances they have been struggling to get out of it. And the majority of the people who did not ask to be in the circumstance are children. The United States of America has experienced several defining events that have challenged us to acknowledge that community and individualism are at least equally important, and that local and global interdependence are imperative (Lee & Hudson, 2017).

At the beginning of this chapter I told you to have an open mind and open heart, and this is the section I was referring to. Pouring peace into our communities can be done in so many different ways. They don't have to be tedious, and they don't have to be expensive either. If you are collaborating with individuals on this task, things such as food drives; summer camps for children; and using individual expertise to educate the community about finances, wealth, gardening, and mental health, and more will be inexpensive. Creating booklets that list local resources and some that are in the surrounding counties will help empower residents to seek out those resources or even create ones that are not available yet. When you are empowering others, especially in the community that helped raised you, that is a noble act. I'm not sure how it makes you feel, but for me it brings me peace knowing that I'm pouring into the community where my story started. The empowerment approach makes connections between social and economic injustice and individual pain and suffering. Utilizing empowerment theory as a unifying framework presents an integrative, holistic approach to meeting the needs of members of oppressed groups (Lee & Hudson, 2017). Peace is found in so many ways. You just needed this book to help guide you in finding them. Sometimes it takes another person to help us see the bigger picture and help bring out the best in us. You can be that person. I know my tone got a little serious there for a second, but Dr. Green came out and I needed that message to be serious.

Solution-Focused Theory

If you are someone that has always been problem-focused instead of solution-focused, this section is for you. We can sit and discuss the problems that we are facing each and every day, but what will that solve? Do you want to be a broken record your entire life? I surely hope not. Get up, go to the record store, and fix it. Pay the price to fix what needs to be fixed. Solution-focused brief therapy SFBT holds clients (aka peace seekers) accountable for solutions rather than problems (Lee, 2017, p. 516). The solution as described by solution-focused therapy is established in the form of a goal that is to be determined and attained by the client (Lee, Uken & Sebold, 2007). In life we are faced with problems most days. That is just the way the world works, unfortunately. But rather than allowing problems to take over us and stress us out every time, let's do something about them. We must stop allowing our issues to steal our joy and take our peace away from us. We all should have established in our brains that problems are just things. They are things that can be fixed easily so we can remain in a peaceful state. I love this theory because it just makes so much sense. Over the years, I have allowed so many bosses to stress me out to the point where I have simply had enough. I sat with myself one day and said, "By forty, I am going to be my own boss, make my own rules, and stress myself out if needed." So now, I am working toward being my own boss daily. That is my solution to that problem. You're probably sitting there wondering, "Is it really that easy?" Yes, friend it really can be that easy to come up with a solution to any problem. It just takes practice. Just imagine being solution focused every time a problem arises. Do you smell the peace, friend? It smells good doesn't it? You don't have to get all stressed with heart palpations. You don't have to knuck if you buck. Things are too high to be bailing you out of jail.

Below is an example that someone I knew was faced with; we'll call him George. I helped George navigate the problem and come up with solutions. And now George is living his best life. George realizes how simple it is to be solution-focused.

Example:

Problem: George complains that his income is not enough to cover his monthly expenses and have money left over. George wants to take lavish trips and ball until he falls. (That's not responsible, but George said it not me)

Solution: George can focus on earning degrees or certificates that will help him get a better job. And then George can be balling out of control (after he pays his bills). George could also advocate for a raise at his current job if he does not want to go to school or obtain a certificate. George could become a leader in his current role to show that he has other skills and that will put him in the running for a potential promotion. Or George could create his own business.

So, instead of George focusing on the problem each day, he can simply go do something about it. Stop meeting up with people that may be experiencing the same thing to discuss the problem. If you are going to meet up with them, change the conversation for once and discuss the vision for your solution instead. Discuss the goals to get to the solution. Start meeting up with people that will help you come up with solutions or motivate you to do so on your own. Put yourself in the best spaces possible to only focus on the solution, friend. It's time you reach your goals and make room for the peace that you deserve. A vision of the ultimate solution without a clear idea of the first small step to achieve it may prove to be too distant and too vague (Lee, 2017). Basically, friend, if you don't have the slightest idea of how you want to solve your problem, then you may feel like it's impossible. Below are statements you can use when you are coming up with solutions. I got you, friend. When I told you way back when to grab my hand and let me guide you, this is exactly what I meant.

Solution-oriented assessment statements (Lee, 2017):

1. There are exceptions to every problem.
2. Language is powerful in creating and sustaining reality. Therefore, the preferred language is the language of solution and change.
3. It is more helpful to focus on what you can do and your strengths than on what you can't do and the problems in the change process.
4. Problems and solutions are your construction; therefore, you will always determine the goals.

Just remember this very simple word going forward, friend: SOLUTION!

Exercise: When you find yourself faced with a problem that is potentially going to get you out of your peaceful state, complete these steps. Please be intentional in the moment.

1. Stop what you are doing.
2. Think about the problem.
3. Is the problem worth getting out of whack for?
4. What absolutely has to be done to solve the problem?
5. Is it even a problem or are you just making it a problem?

Problem:

_____

_____

_____

_____

_____

Solution:

_____

_____

_____

_____

_____

Problem:

_____

_____

_____

_____

_____

_____

Solution:

_____

_____

_____

_____

_____

_____

_____

Problem:

_____

_____

_____

_____

_____

_____

Solution:

_____

_____

_____

_____

_____

_____

_____

_____

Narrative Theory

Narrative theory focuses on helping individuals change how they currently perceive themselves and the things they have been through in life and retell their stories. Just because you have been a certain way your whole life does not mean that must be the story you stick with until you die. Just because you experienced trauma and hardship when you were younger does not mean that has to be the story you tell people who had nothing do with it. White and Epston believe that we all "story" our lives to make sense out of them (Kelly and Smith, 2017). Now while that is true, we don't want our past to prevent us from experiencing a peaceful future. Stories are stories. But let's place the old story on the bookshelf and tell a new one. Out with the old and in with the new. In no way am I saying forget what you have been through, but I do want you to be intentional about being open to receiving peace in ways that you may or may not have thought about before opening this book.

The goal of narrative treatment in social work practice is for clients first to understand and then to broaden and change the stories around which they have organized their lives, and to assess and challenge the socio/cultural political sources that have influenced them (Kelly and Smith, 2017). You are the client here and today you are starting a new story. Repeat after me: "Today starts a new day." Think about truths you have accepted from your family members that have affected you all your life. Really sit and think about your current reality. Is it holding you back? Has it shaped the way you interact with people? Has it been surrounded by poverty? Has it been surrounded by violence? Has it been surrounded by disappointment? Questions like these will help you assess other ways to view a situation, analyze for alternative meanings, and find other aspects of your life, often involving strengths and coping, which may have been lost in the over-focus on problems (Kelly and Smith, 2017). Who says you can't rewrite your story at any point in your life? No one, friend. Rewrite your story the best way you know how and start living a new reality that feels much better.

So, after reading all of that I *hope* you're still not wondering "How does her social work education and inner peace correlate?" But if you are I totally understand and I'll explain, because it's so simple. So, I gave you the definition of inner peace and shared some social work theories with you. I took you to class friend. But did you read? Did you study? The theories that I shared will all help you in your daily life with things that you may be experiencing. If you utilize the approaches, then boom there's inner peace in your life. Use them to help center you. You don't have to do life alone. When life is throwing all sorts of things at you externally, you still remain calm on the inside. These tools will help life become a lot less stressful. Build your toolbox starting today. Having a toolbox in 2025 is where it's at. Class is dismissed for now (until you turn the page).

> *"You have peace," the old woman said, "when you make it with yourself."*
>
> —*Mitch Albom*

CHAPTER 3

Protecting Peace

On a peaceful note......

Peace can be fun in the sun. Peace can be a breeze in the park on a nice sunny spring day. Peace is laughing your behind off at your bestie being crazy. Peace is spending that pocket change to get you a nice, deserved massage. Peace is learning to let that toxic baggage goooooooo. Peace is taking care of YOUR mind, body, and soul. Peace is your peace until it is not.

Now that we discussed how I gained my peace, let's get into how I remain at peace. I'm so excited for this chapter because so many people ask me all the time how I remain in a peaceful state. They have said things such as, "Girl, you are such a peaceful person," "You're full of sunshine," "How do you remain peaceful in such a cold world?" I'm addicted to peace y'all. And I'm addicted real bad. Once you get a taste of it, you'll see how easy it is to remain at peace most times. I'm not saying I don't go through things or stress, but for the most part I am peace and peace is me. I'm sure the snacks and drink you had during chapter 1 are long gone and you're thirsty for something to drink and hungry for this chapter. Go get a refill or a whole meal. I'll wait!

You back? Good. Good food is one of the things that helps keep me peaceful. When I'm out and about, I try to keep me some good ole snacks in the car. A girl gets hungry in traffic sometimes! If you live in Atlanta, you can totally relate. In this chapter I want you to set the atmosphere to a peaceful environment. If you have candles light them. If you have a diffuser, put the lavender drops and mix it with eucalyptus. Thank me later! If you have a beautiful porch, go sit on it. Those are a few things I do to maintain my peace. Just grab something that puts you in the most relaxing mood and cut your phone off. I want you to really take this information in undisturbed. This is me helping you set the tone for what's to come.

Are y'all ready? Here we go.

Remaining at peace is maintenance. The way you maintain the interior and exterior of your car and house is what I do each and every day for my mind, body, and soul. And we all know the maintenance on cars and houses never ever ends. When I wake up every morning, I set a positive mood for my day. I speak positive things in the atmosphere. As I look in the mirror, I say things such as, "Girl you are worthy of peace," "Let's redirect all negative things that come to try to steal your peace," and "You are the driver of your life. No one else can drive your life but you, unless you let them." Once you are fully in control of the steering wheel, it's hard for someone to come and tell you how to drive your life or make you anxious about what is to come. I have a good grip on my wheel, so the devil could sit next to me at the nail salon and tell me that "the world is ending tomorrow." It would be so easy for me to stay peaceful and continue watching the people out the window at the nail salon I go to at the Beltline and sip my margarita and smile.

> "No one else can drive your life but you, unless you let them." Once you are fully in control of the steering wheel, it's hard for someone to come and tell you how to drive your life or make you anxious about what is to come.

And yes, I said sip my margarita. I like to drink a margarita sometimes when I go get my nails and toes done at this beautiful spot on the Beltline. It brings me peace, especially after I've had a long week at work. If you haven't tried it, run don't walk. It is called Lacquer Nail Bar. Thank me later. The Beltline is an area in Atlanta that has nice restaurants, nice apartments, bike and scooter rental options, a park, and a grocery store just to name a few things. The Beltline is family and dog friendly. It's a place I like to go and enjoy time with my family and friends. Being able to walk or ride a bike along the Beltline and look at the beautiful scenery does something to my soul. My soul just got excited just thinking about it. Being outside is so peaceful. Go get you some of that outside peace friend. I promise you won't regret it. If you have never been to a waterfall, you need to go this year. I love going to the waterfall and just listening to the water and all the animals that are nearby. I usually take me some healthy snacks and whatever book I'm reading at the time. Close your eyes for a second and imagine yourself laying on a log, listening to the water, reading a good book, and snacking on some good ole nuts. Doesn't that sound relaxing? I just need to write my name on the log at the Roswell Waterfall because that is my spot. If you're on the log and you see me coming, move please and thank you.

I'm a sucker for a good ole charcuterie board any day of the week. I prefer it to be outside though. Close your eyes again please and thank you. Now just imagine yourself sitting outside at a park or balcony with a charcuterie board full of your favorite treats. I know you felt that nice breeze. Imagine you took a bite of that gouda cheese and those crackers. Didn't that feel like peace in that moment? Well, I spare no funds when it comes to building the perfect board to enjoy out in nature. Charcuterie boards are the perfect way to bring people together. I usually eat charcuterie with my other best friend Asha. We eat, laugh so hard that we start crying, and talk about all the things. I love adding aged cheeses, nuts, assortment crackers, olives, fruit, and beef bites. And don't let Kirkland's or Hobby Lobby have a good sale; I'm going to get more charcuterie boards. You're probably wondering, how many boards does one need? Well, if you're the hostess with the mostest, you need a plethora. Don't judge me. Now go get you some and thank me later.

Staying true to myself allows me to maintain peace as well. I'm from Macon and proud of it. I love to walk around my dad's front yard barefoot. Just the front yard though. The backyard and I have a love-hate relationship. Stepping in too many ant beds growing up will scar you for life. I've been in Atlanta now since 2018 and I love the culture. But not allowing the city life to change me into something that I am not is peaceful. Not many people can move from their country hometown and not become a whole different person.

I was raised in a Baptist church where the pastor preached all day and I had to sit in the front pew. And don't let my bigma see me playing with my cousins or not putting the dollar she gave me in the collection plate. She would get us together after church in such a nice way. Learning the bible and how good God is was something I did not take seriously as a young girl, but as I've gotten older, I've been able to understand the Lord's word better. When I was a young girl, I knew it was important because my bigma said so just about every day. She bought my siblings and me our own individual bibles. She even ordered us a collection of bible story books meant for children from a commercial. Those books are still at my dad's house today. I appreciate her effort in making sure we knew the Lord.

Now that I am older, I have time to break down every chapter in my own timing and way. Allowing that seed that was planted in me at such a young age to flourish protects my peace. Utilizing different bible stories for daily life challenges has shown me that

> Praying and resting in the prayer is peaceful.

God is the way and nothing less. I go to the Lord in prayer most times instead of being anxious about life situations. When I go to him in prayer, I ask specifically for what I need and also show gratitude for what God has done for me. Praying and resting in the prayer is peaceful. Y'all have to read that again. Praying and resting in the prayer is peaceful. Y'all gone make me preach up in here! We will save that for later though.

I'm sure you've heard of code-switching before. If you haven't, code-switching is when there is a shift from one language or dialect to another, depending on the social context or conversation setting.

Basically, when a person is in a certain setting and if they change their normal language to please other people, they are code-switching. I explained that to say, truly being myself in all settings is peaceful. Studies show that people who code-switch deal with mental health issues. It burns people out from having to be something they are not all day. When I'm at work of course I'm professional, but I'm not going to change my voice to sound like any other race. What you see and hear is what you get. Most times, I'm using the same slang that I use at home at work. Slang is embedded in today's society. I've had conversations with doctors, CEOs, and other professionals, and they use slang at times too. As long as I'm not cursing or being disrespectful, let me be me. I remember telling one of the doctors I work with "I'll holla at you later." And to my surprise he responded and said, "Stay up homie." He probably said that because he knew how stressful my job can get. I had one medical director that was so cool, he would always call me "sis" and he was my "big bro."

Be you in all spaces, respectfully and unapologetically. If I'm ever anxious at work, it's because of complex situations or something that I am dealing with at home. I will never be anxious because of me trying to be someone I am not. If you catch me talking like Karen, then something is wrong. And I beg you to please call me out on it. Let's normalize speaking up when someone you know very well has just switched up their voice right in front of you. It doesn't have to be in a mean or disrespectful way. You can simply say something such as "You sound different today; what's going on?" Or just remind the person that they are dope just the way they are if you don't want to get into a whole conversation about it. You were created the way you were because that's how you are supposed to operate. The Big Homie (aka God) created all things with intention and differentially. Embrace that. Rest in that.

We care way too much about what others think of us and the decisions we decide to make in today's society. God made me this way for a reason, so I'm sticking beside it. It is none of my concern that the person sitting next to me at the doctor's office thinks my shoes are ugly. I saw them at the store, I loved them, and I purchased them with my hard-working money. I got away from letting people place their insecurities on me. People will have you thinking you have on the ugliest shoes, clothes, and that you are not *that* girl or guy. And guess what? You are indeed *that* girl or guy. I'm at peace with all my purchases, hairstyles, and decisions. I am that girl. And that girl that is at peace with who she is. Period! It is important to ask other's opinions when needed, but don't ever get to a point where you are taking what someone said and running with it each time. Remember, you are the driver of your life, so do what will help you sleep great at night.

Wellness has become such a huge part of my life. Getting massages, foot detoxes, facials; having a skincare routine; and keeping up with my annual health appointments (just to name a few) are significant. You may have read that and seen too many dollar signs. Trust me all the dollar signs are so worth it. We do not work just to pay bills. Spending money to take care of my body is always top priority. When you treat your body right, it does what it needs to do. Am I wrong? Not at all.

When I get my massages, I like to be *beat*. Apply all the pressure you can to my body because I'm sure it needs all of it. Being diagnosed with psoriatic arthritis has also made me take wellness more seriously than before. It causes a lot of joint pain mostly. Having it, I've had to make many life adjustments, and that's okay. Staying on top of things such as foot detoxes help get toxins out of my body, reducing inflammation. They do such wonders that my fiancé bought me a foot detox kit to use at home. Shoutout to Troy y'all. I just love that handsome man. He is peace too. (At the end of this book I'm going to place a list of things that you can utilize for wellness.)

My skin used to be terrible growing up, so I made myself a promise. As soon as I got a little pocket change, I would get my skin together. (My grandfather used to always call it pocket change growing up and I just love the saying, but back to my skin.) Y'all, it was so bad that it caused a lot of anxiety and shame. At one point my face looked like a connect the dot puzzle. There were pimples everywhere. Your girl got connected with one of the best estheticians in Atlanta and hasn't looked back since. Having great skin that glows and is blemish free is peace. As soon as my esthetician's hands hit my face, there was calm and peace in knowing that things would only get better from there. My confidence is at an all-time high now. I no longer feel the need to wear a lot of makeup or not take close-up pictures. To maintain my clear skin, I practice a skin care routine for morning and night. My esthetician has his own skin care line, so I bought all the products necessary. Were they cheap? Absolutely not. The cheap products I was buying from Walmart were not getting the job done at all. It takes a lot of discipline to maintain a peaceful life, but once you get into your own groove and start to really love the feeling of peace, the maintenance will be second nature to you.

Some people don't believe in science and prefer to take care of their health in a natural manner. That is totally fine; do what works for you. I believe in science and natural remedies when it comes to my health. Every year I get my annual eye exam, physical, pap smear, and dental checkup just to name a few. It helps my anxiety remain low when I know that I am healthy. And if something shows up on a test and it is an abnormality, I can do what needs to be done to correct it. Preventative care is what you call it. Close your eyes for a second and just be aware of your body and how it feels in this moment. Think about the last time you went to the doctor. Think about stories you hear online or from a loved one about how they waited too late to go to the doctor. Was there some anxiety there? If so run, don't walk to your medical doctor or holistic doctor. I feel in control knowing that I checked off those boxes, so I don't have to think about whether my health is in good standing or not. As I typed this line I smiled because I have been through a lot in these thirty-three years, but I've made it and persevered each and every time. When I say I have been through a lot that's an understatement.

Back in 2016, I was driving down Eisenhower Parkway in Macon, and my face started to hurt so bad. I was worried because I had never felt anything like that before. I was not in control of my health. I called my oldest sister Crystal, and we went to urgent care as soon as we could. The doctors completed all the routine procedures and took some blood as well. When the doctor came back in the room, she explained that I tested positive for Lyme disease. I had no clue what that was. The doctor explained that it is when you get bitten by an infected tick out in wooded areas. During that time, I rarely spent time in areas that were heavily wooded. I was at a loss for words. I had to take antibiotics for a while and get tested every so often. After some time, my tests started to come back negative. Thank God. Just imagine if I ignored that facial pain and wrote it off as nothing. I could have possibly been crippled for the rest of my life. The bacteria, which is called borrelia, can leave you with serious long-term effects. Dealing with the disease was no easy feat because most days, I did not know what to expect. There were days my entire body hurt so bad; it took me a while just to walk to my car. I also had short-term memory loss, sleep deprivation, and more. I shared this story to say that if you feel something, do something about it.

Now that's my story about how I protect my peace. You sit tight because we are going to work together to start you on your journey.

> *"Peace is a journey of a thousand miles and it must be taken one step at a time."*
>
> —*Lyndon B. Johnson*

CHAPTER 4

Peaceful Mechanisms

On a Peaceful Note......

Peace is what you make it. Peace is creative. Peace is exciting. Peace can be tied up in a little bow. Peace is writing. Peace is therapy. Peace is family. Peace is a seafood boil in moderation. (Had to add moderation.) Peace is cheeks in the sand on the beach. Peace is dancing in the rain. Peace is sweating toxins out during Pilates.

*P**eaceful mechanisms* help you create peace in your everyday life. I'm sure you have heard of coping mechanisms, so I decided to put a twist on it and create peaceful mechanisms. In this chapter there will be an ample number of resources for you to refer to whenever your heart desires. I'm sure you have several things already in place (or maybe not) that bring you peace, but these are some things you may not have thought of. These are things, places, and people that bring me the utmost peace, and sharing is caring friend. This chapter is full of more tools for your toolbox. You can use these resources daily, monthly, or yearly. Peace is found in so many ways, and this chapter should be used as the catalyst to get to where you want to be on the peace spectrum (which I made up). Do what works for you, friend. Take as many or few as you need and thank me later.

Environment

Nature

Being out in nature does not excite everyone and that is ok. We were all created differently. Don't underestimate the power of nature, though. Give it a chance. Get you some natural bug repellent and just go. Look up your closest park, mountains, waterfall, beach, or trail. Some of my favorite places to go to connect with nature and learn lessons from are Roswell Waterfall, Stone Mountain, Beltline, Gibbs Garden, the botanical garden, and numerous parks around Atlanta. And if you are wondering how one can learn lessons from nature, just go and sit long enough. If you sit long enough and stay present, you will learn to appreciate nature more and more. Nature taught me that regardless of what snowstorm or thunderstorm comes its way, it will forever be resilient and show up in its original state at some point. Go smell the roses and learn about different plants and animals.

Diffusers

When you are in a room that feels and smells like heaven, is that not peaceful? You don't have to purchase the most expensive diffuser unless you want something that is aesthetically pleasing and meshes well with your décor. Diffusers can be purchased at Target, TJ Maxx, Marshalls, and Amazon. Now once you decide on your diffuser, get your essentials oils. My perfect blend is lavender and eucalyptus. Please mix those two at some point and thank me later. There are other oils too such as tea tree, peppermint, and rosemary, just to name a few. Get you a few to start out with and put your diffuser in a place where you spend the most time. Putting it in a room where you spend a lot of time guarantees you will give it an honest try. Imagine coming home from a long day of work pouring yourself a glass of your favorite wine and cutting on your diffuser to decompress from the day. Sounds like a mini spa at home to me.

Experiences

Start a book club

Reading is not only fundamental, but it is an outlet. It gives you a chance to shut out the world and think about something else for a while. And why not discuss the book with a group of people. You are not only discussing a book that you all enjoy, but you are building a community to lean on when life is stressful. I'm not saying you have to go tell the book club all of your personal business, but there may be a few people in the group you can relate to and build a friendship with. There is a book club in Atlanta called the "Silent Book Club" that is pretty dope. Check to see if one is offered in your city. The first time I went I truly enjoyed it, because the book I read, *Power Moves* by Sarah Jakes Roberts, was what my soul needed that day after work. Silence was needed too, to recharge. The way the book club works is you meet at the chosen location for that session, bring a book, and read. You have the option to discuss your book at the end or not. But silence is key.

Food

Food has gone up in price drastically since the 1970s. Wouldn't it be nice to be able to leave out the grocery store with 100 items for $50. Maybe we will get back there one day. Let me be optimistic for just a second please. Food is something we can't survive without at all. We tend to purchase food that we can afford. I totally understand. And a lot of times the foods we buy are not good for us. To ensure that you are consuming items that won't cause some of the major diseases such as cancer, heart failure, and diabetes, we must make some sacrifices. Cutting down or out expenses in some areas in your life so you have more good food, if you are able, may be the best idea. Putting quality food in your body is necessary. We have to eat to live.

Since I make more money now, I don't mind shopping at places such as Trader Joes, Whole Foods, and Sprouts. You can even get some healthy options at Kroger. But quality food is peace. When you eat good, you feel good. Let me say that again. *When you eat good, you feel good.* Now I'm not saying to deprive yourself of that big fat juicy burger every once or twice a year. But try implementing more healthy foods than toxic ones. Meal prepping and juicing are some things I have adopted so I can make sure I am eating and drinking healthy. And treat yourself to a good ole restaurant every now and then. I *love* a restaurant with a top-tier experience. Atlas in Atlanta is 10/10, friend. The experience starts at the door. They put so much love in the greeting. "Hey, welcome in. Is there anything I can get for you? Let us know." Whew! I just walked in. The bread service will make you melt to the floor. And paired with the butter that is always locally made tops it off every time. All this to say: good food—at home or in a restaurant—means a good experience and peace.

Day Spas

Going to my first day spa was one of the best decisions I could have ever made. Being able to spend half or a whole day at a place of calmness and relaxation is peace. You will have to pay to get inside the facility and then you will have to pay for your services separately. Most of the day spas offer services such as massages, body scrubs, facials, hair washing, and restaurants. You don't typically have to pay extra for the saunas, pools, hot tubs, and lounge areas. The last time I went to a day spa in Virginia, I spent $300 and I would do it again. My body from head to toe felt so refreshed. Remember, we are thinking outside of our normal routine of self-care. Go to the spa and let them beat on you and thank me later. When your body feels good, so does the mind.

Different States/Countries

When is the last time you left the state you currently live in? If you take forever to think about this question, then go ahead and get online and plan you a quick trip. If you don't have a lot of PTO, then take you a weekend trip. Don't be like me and take PTO that you don't have. Whew it is hard getting out of the negative. But think of a place that you have always wanted to go outside of your origin state or country. It is so much out there to explore. Pack a light bag, find you some reasonably priced tickets, and just gooooo. Don't think too long about it because you may change your mind. Your body and mind need new scenery and education. One of the best places I could have ever gone is the Dominican Republic. Going there and interacting with the locals taught me to just be happy no matter what I have or don't have. I have never in life seen so many happy people in one place. Everyone greeted us with smiles everywhere we went. I met someone that was so nice, he up and left his job one day to escort us to a restaurant. The DR taught me to not move so fast (even though I still tend to move fast—I'm a work in progress, y'all.) The DR also taught me to choose quality everything. I indulged in some of the best drinks and food. Remember we are here for a good time not a long time, and we want to make sure it is a peaceful one.

The Country

If you already live in the country kudos to you because it is so peaceful. Being in the country away from the busy city life is needed sometimes. I go to my brother's home not only to spend time with him and his family but also to experience peace and quiet. Just imagine walking around chasing chickens and cuddling with bunnies. That could be you. Kick your feet up on the porch, as us southerners say, and get you a glass of sweet tea, wine, or water. Sounds pretty serene to me. Go on a walk through the fields of vegetables and fruit and smell the freshness. Walk barefoot and experience earthing. Sometimes all you need is a touch of the grass.

I WOKE UP AND CHOSE PEACE

Relationships

Family/Friends

After God, family and friends are the most important people in our lives. Now they can work our nerves at times, but we end up talking to them the next day or week. Utilize them to help make your life more peaceful. When you are going through tough times, call them or meet up with them. Just being around my family brings me peace. We can be sitting in the same room on our phones not saying anything to each other. Just having them in my presence is enough sometimes. They are my safe haven. And to my family that is reading this, yes, I said you are my safe heaven, meat head. Meat head was something that my late uncle Lyria used to call my siblings, cousin, and myself. (Now he was really a safe haven).

Therapist

Now don't you skip over this section. Like I mentioned previously, "you might not like the idea of putting someone else in your business." But trust me, it is something you should try if needed. Your therapist does not know you from anywhere unless they're a family member or friend, so go to a therapist that does not know you from anywhere. Therapists are not there to judge you at all. They are there to help you sort out your issues and cope better.

Remember how I said one of my clients had me rapping? I had to do what I had to do for her. If you get you a therapist that you feel comfortable with and let them know what you need to progress, they just might get on the track with you. Remember, closed mouths don't get fed, friend.

Mentors

We all know someone that has or had the same goals as us and works in the similar field as us or a different field as us. I have met people along my career journey and asked them to become my mentors. None of us knows it all, and we probably will never know it all. Having someone that you can meet up with to talk to about career stuff (or just life in general), is necessary to gain perspectives and advice that may help you get ahead and reach your goals.

Pastor

I'm sure you have heard of the saying, "Go to the Lord in prayer." Well, go to the pastor and ask for prayer and guidance. The pastor is the pastor for a reason. He or she is placed in their role to work on behalf of the Lord. They utilize their platform to interpret the bible for God's people. If you are in need of a personalized session to understand the word better or need to gain some peace, GO TO THE PASTOR!

Time with Self

Objects

There are many hats you can wear as a social worker. And one of the hats is a therapist. I loved helping people with their issues and giving them tools to handle stressors. For example, I had a list of objects that I would send clients who preferred something in their hand to cope with anxiety and stress. If you are someone that deals with a lot of stress during the day, then consider implementing objects to help reduce the stress: fidget toys such as slime balls, spinner toys, squishy cubes, and balls made of gel or soft clay. Massage devices just feel so good after a long day. They are cost efficient too. Go on Amazon, and search for a few, and get one that calls out to you, "Get me, get me." My fiancé let me borrow his massage gun and I have yet to return it. Technically, it's mine too. We are about to become one soon. But get you a massage gun or something similar and massage those muscles. Who said you can only get a good massage at the spa?

One thing I love about my fiancé is he makes sure I have all the self-care gadgets. Not only did he buy me a foot detox kit, which I mentioned earlier, but he bought me some hot stones too. Close your eyes for a second. Just imagine taking you a nice ole bubble bath with your favorite candle going and a book in hand. Preferably this book. After you get out the bubble bath your hot stones are hot and ready. You let your partner put some oil on your back and rub the stones until they are no longer hot. OMG! Let's not stop there. If you're anything like me, I have to take a shower after my bath because I was just sitting in my dirt. Ew. Let the toxins pull from your feet and hop in the shower with your favorite scrub. You just had a spa day for free 99. That was a lot I know. That's why you make time for things as such. When you know you're going to be off of work or just start early one evening when you get off to allow time to truly enjoy the experience. You don't have to always go to the spa to get receive spa treatment. Just use the objects you have.

Pottery

If you've ever done pottery before, you know it involves a lot of focusing in that moment. You especially have to focus if you want your piece to be molded perfectly. Pottery allows you to shut out the world. I am trying to be intentional about being present in the moment these days. If you want to practice being present more, start with pottery. While you're participating in pottery, you have to pay attention to how fast your clay is spinning and what shape you are forming. This activity will be the start of you being present more and not worrying yourself about what is going on in the world or the future so much. Get those hands dirty!

Writing

Writing is a major peaceful outlet. Get you a designated journal and your favorite pen and just start. Start writing and see how it feels to you. We don't always want to talk, so let your pen do the talking for you. Who knows, this may be the start of you becoming a *New York Times best-selling* author. See how I'm speaking that out there for you. I want nothing but the best for you, friend. Write until you can't write anymore. Write until your hands hurt. But don't knock it until you try it. You could write about things such as your feelings from the day, problems and solutions, dreams, short stories, or whatever you are interested in at the time.

Crafts

We all have some type of creative bone in our bodies. Take some time away from your phone or another bad habit you can think of. Give yourself space and the opportunity to tap into your creative side. What projects do you enjoy seeing other people do on TV or around town? It doesn't have to be expensive unless you want it to be. When I was a little girl, I would find materials around my bigma's house to create whatever came to my little mind. In doing this it not only gives you the opportunity to tap into that creative side, but it can help boost your self-esteem. If you complete one project and feel great about it, you may want to do more. If you weren't sure about your abilities before your project, I hope you are after. This could be the start of something great, such as a business. And then boom, you have brought in more peace than you have ever had. Business = more money. More money = financial freedom. Financial freedom = peace. See what I just did there?

Books

If you are a reader like me, you can relate when I say that a good ole book can bring you a sense of calmness. Don't just limit yourself to books that you have read since you were younger. There are so many genres of books such as contemporary fiction, drama, fantasy, science fiction, and romance, just to name a few. Expand your reading palate. Take a trip to Barnes & Noble or a smaller bookstore if you are big on supporting small businesses. Explore the book sections and read the descriptions on the backs of the books. What I have started doing is finding books that go perfectly with the season. For example, during the fall I read a book called *The Pumpkin Spice Café,* and it was such a cozy read. Imagine yourself during the fall cuddled up in a blanket, with your book, and a pumpkin spice latte in hand. During the summer of 2024 I read a book called *Summer's Gift* because it was summertime. It was a cute romance book that opened my reading palate to the romance genre. Whew! Sounds like a good ole time to me. And don't forget reading is just flat out fundamental.

Rest

Sometimes all you need is rest. Rest in knowing that you're being productive when you are resting. You are restoring your body, soul, and mental from a long week or day. Stop feeling like you need to be productive every second of the day. Your nervous system deserves to just lay and do nothing. Imagine how your nervous system must feel being on the go every second of the day. Take time to slow down and rest.

Movement

Yoga

Your girl just recently started yoga and I absolutely love it. I started a yoga event with two amazing ladies where we try to meet each month. We call it yoga and healing. We have the ladies bring their journals, so after yoga we can all write about how it made us feel and our healing journey. Yoga has so many benefits, including helping with pain, relaxation, flexibility, and stress management, just to name a few. Remember, one of the goals to maintaining your peace is reducing your stress levels.

Work Out

Move that body. Get those limbs and muscles going. Go at your own pace. Do not look around and try to keep up with Jim the body builder. Remember, Jim is a body builder and he is true to that not new to that. Figure out what you need to work on. Once you realize what is driving you crazy to look at every day, start there. Get you a gym membership and research all the amenities they offer. If you're paying for a membership monthly, why not get everything you can out of it? I love the gyms that have massage beds in them. After doing all that hard work, one deserves to get a massage. Now make sure you educate yourself on the equipment you use. I would hate for you to be posted on Tik Tok or Instagram looking crazy because you are using the equipment wrong. If you are tired of a traditional membership, seek out alternatives such as Pilates. I have become a Pilates girl myself. Work it on out, friend.

Dance

Dance it out, friend. It does not matter if you can or cannot. Have a dance party in your room or somewhere in the house. Take a dance class or two. Dancing will help you feel free. Just move to the beat. My friend Mareena is a dancer, and she loves it. She says that "Through dance, I process emotions that I do not always have words for." It's a sacred place that helps her quiet her mind, release stuck energy, boost her confidence, and feel whole again. Dance reminds her that peace lives inside her; she just has to move to find it.

> "You have everything you need for complete peace and total happiness right now."
> —Wayne W. Dyer

CHAPTER 5

Your Turn to Write.
Reflection Time.

ASHLEY GREEN, LMSW

This chapter is you for you to reflect on what you have read in the last few chapters. Go back and read it all if you need to, but take this chapter seriously. Think about only yourself. What does peace look like to you? What could bring you peace? What is not peaceful? You can also answer the questions that were in chapter 1 in this chapter. Remember, my journey is my journey and your journey is your journey. We have lived different lives all of our lives. We may relate on certain situations, but at the end of the day, you are your own individual with different experiences and expectations. Use my words and experiences as a guide to how you would want your peaceful journey to look starting today. I believe in you and your capabilities. And so should you. You have what it takes to open the door for peace. You deserve peace and all that it brings. You deserve to glow and grow. Peace would look so good on you and I really want that for you. So write your little heart away. Ready set gooooooo.

_____

_____

_____

_____

_____

_____

_____

_____

_____

_____

_____

_____

_____

_____

_____

_____

_____

_____

_____

_____

_____

CHAPTER 6

Peace in Thy Home

On a peaceful note......

*Peace is a feeling. Peace is a look. Peace can be a smell.
Peace is functional. Peace is when you open the front
door of your home and feel safe and serene.*

For the longest, I underestimated how you can create a peaceful home. If you're wondering how that is possible, wonder no more. A lot of times we purchase a home or rent an apartment and leave it at that. You spend so much money on down payments and deposits that after all of that, you don't want to spend another dime. Trust me, I get it friend, from the bottom of my heart. In this chapter, let me help you realize how you can create a peaceful space. Let me help you wake up to peace friend. This chapter will be an interactive chapter. So be prepared to get up and move around. Let's be partners in this process.

Just take a moment and really think about how your home looks and if it brings you joy or motivates you to do better in life. If you're wondering how home décor equals doing better in life, you'll understand after you read this chapter.

> Is your home dark? Does your home stink? Is your home dirty? Is your home disorganized? Is your home just flat out boring?

Is your home dark? Does your home stink? Is your home dirty? Is your home disorganized? Is your home just flat out boring? If you answered yes to any of those questions, friend, please keep reading this chapter and take it seriously. How can you truly have peace if your home is a disaster? You can't! You are just managing right now. You are just getting by. You are just tolerating your space. That ends today, friend. I'm not saying go out and spend your life savings to change your space. What I am saying is create you a plan to switch things up. Now, if you have plenty of money to spend, just throw it in the bag. It's time to spice things up. Once you have a plan mapped out you can figure out what it is you want to do differently to create a space that will cheer you up after a long day of work. The longer you wait, the longer you will have those dark walls all over the house that do not fit your personality. I can talk interior design all day (and even in my sleep), so holla if you need me.

Don't be like me and get overwhelmed because you are trying to do too many rooms at once. Not only was I physically and emotionally overwhelmed when I started working on my home, but my pockets were overwhelmed. Start small and work your way up. I started with my home office and bedroom at the same time, and it was a lot. I had to really think about what room I needed to be more functional right away. And it was my office. Whew! I know my family and friends got tired of me talking about it.

The reason it had to be designed first was because I needed a motivating space to work where I could go in and stay in for hours. If you are a designer or a writer, you know what I mean. We can't just create in any ole space. My home office is part of the reason this book is completed. Deciding on the wall color was the hardest, because I wanted it to reflect me and my needs, but it couldn't be too dark. When walls are too dark, they don't motivate you to work. Sometimes when I go somewhere and the walls are too dark, I want to relax and sleep. Some lounges and bars have dark walls that aren't too dark and, most times, they are cute. They motivate me to chill with my friends, catch up, and even drop it low a few times. But I hope you get the point. When deciding on wall colors, a lot of thought must be put into it for motivation, relaxation, and entertainment purposes. Most importantly you want to ensure that it does not clash with your décor in that room. Just imagine painting all your walls in your living room hot pink. Next to those hot pink walls you have a beautiful modern cream couch, a clear coffee table with designer books and a small tray that sits under the books. There is also an accent chair that complements your couch and with the best material attached. I'm going to stop there because that would just give me a headache each and every day. To each their own, though. Wall colors *matter* friend. You want to make sure that the walls not only complement your nice furniture but also gives you that feeling of relaxation and *peace.*

Go to your local home improvement store and have a blast. Take you as many sample swatches as you need. That's what they are there for. At most, if not all, home improvement stores, you can buy small cans of sample for as low as $5. Buy the samples and paint small swatches on your wall. Live with the colors for a few days and decide what colors stand out to you the most. What colors made you feel warm inside? What colors made you feel like a million bucks? If you are renting an apartment, ask about painting the walls before you start. Or if you couldn't care less about those rules or that deposit, *turn up!* (But don't go telling your leasing manager that I said that. Don't throw your girl under the bus.) And if you really want to spice your walls up, add an accent wall. I added an accent wall with floral wallpaper in my office. It turned out to be the best decision. With that accent wall, I chose to paint the other three walls hunter green. I was torn between a purple or a pink, but after giving it careful thought, the green made more sense because it complimented the floral wallpaper perfectly. It will be easier to still use if I want to switch the décor up in the office, and it was not too light or too dark for my mood needs.

My office is functional in every way that I need it to be. Your girl gets down in that office. Every time I go in there, I get excited. My toes just start wiggling and feel ready to protect my peace. And that's what I want for you. That office has become my prayer room, yoga studio, club, and much more. Painting the walls was also therapeutic for me. I cut my record player on and just relaxed as I stroked. I remember one day I had my Prince record going with a glass of red wine and just got lost in my thoughts. During that session I was very calm and I made sound decisions due to my calm state. Peaceful space = calm mind and body = better decisions. Remember, you can always find peace in the simple things.

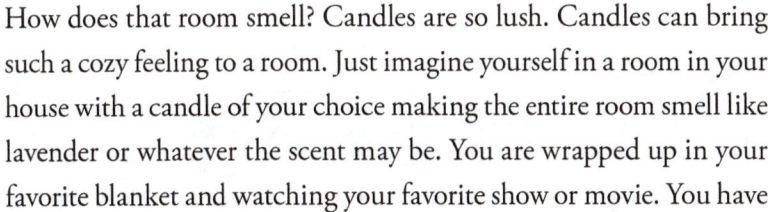

Peaceful space=calm mind and body=better decisions. Remember, you can always find peace in the simple things.

Decorative Pieces

Who doesn't love a beautiful staple peace? Don't just go into a store and buy pieces because they are cute. Buy what really speaks to you. Buy what makes you happy. Buy pieces that are meaningful to you. Buy pieces that will spark an interesting and fun conversation with your guest. Buy pieces with sayings on them that will help start your day off right. I bet you're thinking buying everything will make you happy, but stay focused, friend. Buy what will complement the décor you already have in the room that the piece is intended for. Doing this will help keep the room on track for completion. After you have bought decorative pieces and things start to bring peace to you, don't stop there.

Scent

How does that room smell? Candles are so lush. Candles can bring such a cozy feeling to a room. Just imagine yourself in a room in your house with a candle of your choice making the entire room smell like lavender or whatever the scent may be. You are wrapped up in your favorite blanket and watching your favorite show or movie. You have a snack and drink nearby. Now that, my friend, is peace. Get natural candles if you can to protect yourself from all the terrible chemicals that some candles have. A good scent can go a long way especially after a long day of work. Certain scents are meant to bring calmness, reduce stress and anxiety. Lavender calms and citrus energizes.

Lighting 💡

If your lighting is terrible, how can you see the room that you are trying to enjoy? Get you some nice light fixtures with the best bulbs that will bring in just enough light for you and your family. If you want to be spicy, get you some lights that you can dim if needed. Set you a nice mood from time to time. Imagine sitting in your kitchen with your girlfriends with the lights dimmed. You have prepared a nice charcuterie board and drinking the finest wine. That is peace and you can't tell me otherwise. Quality time and laughter = peace. You could also use those lights for a nice dinner with le boo boo. Instead of going to your favorite restaurant, bring it home. Order from the restaurant, set your table with your finest dinnerware and dim those lights. Boom! Your kitchen is your new favorite restaurant. Some people need bright lights to control their moods. If you are someone that has been diagnosed with depression or anxiety, having bright lights may help with your mood alongside other things. Blue and green lights, just to name a couple, may help with anxiety and depression.

Plants 🍀

Now while you are at the home improvement store, push your cart right on around to the plant section. Look around and see what stands out to you the most. Smell the plants because you will have that scent in your home. A lot of times we purchase plants because they are beautiful, and nothing is wrong with that at all. But let's also do our research and google plants that have the greatest benefits to us and that will last long. Plants offer benefits such as purifying the air, lowering levels of carbon dioxide, inspiring you to eat heathier, reducing stress, and healing. It only takes a few minutes to search the best plants or ask a team member at the store. Though, you are probably better off searching on your phone. A lot of the time the store's team members will respond and say, "Oh I don't know, I just work here." Save yourself the trouble and do your research before you go or ask someone that specializes in plants. Some plants that are worth considering are spider plants, snake plants, succulents, peace lilies, ferns, different herbs, and pothos. Pick one of those plants, or others you research, and place them wherever your heart desires. I'm a nature lover, so being around certain plants brings me a sense of calm. Who doesn't love greenery? Adding plants to a room is always the perfect finishing touch. Friend, you can have both: a cute plant and a plant with health and peace benefits.

Bedding

One hundred dollars for bedding? Yes! Try to be mindful of what matters to you when purchasing your bedding. If you are going to spend less on bedding, make sure the quality is good. You deserve to live like a Queen or King. Imagine going to bed every night and laying on itchy bedding. That is so not peace, friend. Go to some of the best home goods stores, look around, and ask questions if needed. Some of the best places to purchase bedding from, in my opinion, are Amazon, Macy's, Belk, and JCPenney. Peace is coming home after a long day of work (or a long day of whatever), showering, and jumping on comfortable bedding. You see I mention showering first because the ancestors would roll over in their graves if we came from outside and sat on our beds with outside clothes on. If you know, you know. Comfortable bedding just makes you want to wiggle your toes uncontrollably and roll in your blanket until you're a burrito. Choose bedding that goes well with the theme that you are going for in your bedroom as well. Please keep that in mind to maintain some order in the room. You want to be proud of your room and want to spend time in there to recharge.

Furniture

As I've gotten older, I've shifted toward a minimalist style in my bedroom. The bedroom is where I rise and unwind. It would cause me great anxiety to have a lot of furniture or things surrounding me every day and I don't want that for you, friend. Back in the day we were so excited about going to the furniture store and getting a whole bedroom set because it consisted of so many pieces of furniture. You had your bed, two nightstands, tall dresser, dresser with the mirror attached, and sometimes a chest at the end of the bed. Whew! I have a bed without a headboard because it is an adjustable bed and a dresser with a mirror attached. Just imagine a room free of clutter where you are not bumping into furniture everywhere you turn. A room where you can have a nice picnic at the foot of your bed with light snacks (*not a seafood boil*), candles, and wine if you chose. I'm a romantic person, so things like that feed my soul. If you are going to add furniture to your room, think about the functionality of the piece first. Don't get overwhelmed thinking about it all but do think about change to welcome overdue peace in your space.

Organization 🧺

Organization is a thing we should all be practicing to remain sane. Just imagine being a mother who has children that are school aged who play sports during the week and weekend and being unorganized. The first thing you probably see in your mind is chaos, right? That is the first thing I see. There are so many stores that you can utilize for storage containers, baskets, calendars, and all the things that you need to stay organized. A few of my favorite places to shop are Amazon and the Container Store. Run, don't walk, to your closest store. I've only experienced aunthood so far in life, so I have not had the pleasure of organizing for children. But having things organized reduces my anxiety, because I know where everything is and that helps me complete tasks that I already don't want to do much easier. Something I love saying to people is "Home is where the heart is." Your home is your sacred place, so remember to always treat it as such. Organize your home and place things in their proper place, as I always say.

My fiancé and I were chatting as I was brainstorming how to get the Peace Seekers (that's y'all) involved during this chapter. We were sitting in the living room, and he asked me what I would rate the room out of 100. I gave it a solid 80. I gave it an 80 because there were so many things missing. I don't have art on the walls, the TV is super small, and there's no entry way table. It just doesn't scream peace and it is not at its maximum functionality. Functionality = peace. Rating the room was a great idea and that led me to start rating other rooms in my home. I wanted to ensure that I was creating the feeling I wanted and that it was also functioning in a way that room should.

Peace Scale ☮

During this next part of the chapter, you are going to rate your rooms on the Peace Scale (yes, I totally just made that up). You probably already knew that was coming though, friend. Rate the room's as maximum or least. Or if it's somewhere in the middle or almost at the max and just needs that one thing to push it to the top, rate it as moderate. Circle your answer as you evaluate each room.

Example Peace Scale

Maximum functionality   Moderate functionality   Least functionality

I want you to walk around your entire home, and pretty please, take your time. Observe and take inventory in every single room. Don't forget your outside area if you have one. Take a few deep breaths and take the room in for a minute. Lay in the room, sip some wine in the room, dance in the room, or pray in the room. Just be in the moment in the room. There are sections on the following pages for you to write in and break down your observations of each room. There are questions to help you figure it all out. I told you a long time ago: I got you. I hope you truly believe that at this point. I am your tour guide. Because truth be told, when it comes to interior design, a lot of people just don't know where to start. And people also tend not to realize that peace can be found in interior design. Raise your hand if that's you, friend. No judgement here at all. Let this chapter be your answer to the chaos you may or may not be experiencing in your home. Let's get started.

Entry Way

Peace Scale

Maximum functionality   **Moderate functionality**   **Least functionality**

1. How does it feel to you?

_____

_____

_____

_____

_____

2. How does it look to you?

_____

_____

_____

_____

_____

3. What can be added?

_____

_____

_____

_____

_____

_____

4. What can be subtracted?

_____

_____

_____

_____

_____

_____

_____

Living Room

Peace Scale

Maximum functionality   **Moderate functionality**   **Least functionality**

1. How does it feel to you?

_____

_____

_____

_____

_____

2. How does it look to you?

_____

_____

_____

_____

_____

_____

3. What can be added?

_____

_____

_____

_____

_____

_____

4. What can be subtracted?

_____

_____

_____

_____

_____

_____

_____

Kitchen

Peace Scale

Maximum functionality   **Moderate functionality**   **Least functionality**

1. How does it feel to you?

_____

_____

_____

_____

_____

2. How does it look to you?

_____

_____

_____

_____

_____

3. What can be added?

_____

_____

_____

_____

_____

_____

4. What can be subtracted?

_____

_____

_____

_____

_____

_____

_____

Pantry

Peace Scale

Maximum functionality   **Moderate functionality**   **Least functionality**

1. How does it feel to you?

_____

_____

_____

_____

_____

2. How does it look to you?

_____

_____

_____

_____

_____

_____

3. What can be added?

_____

_____

_____

_____

_____

_____

4. What can be subtracted?

_____

_____

_____

_____

_____

_____

_____

Master Suite

Peace Scale

Maximum functionality   **Moderate functionality**   **Least functionality**

1. How does it feel to you?

_____

_____

_____

_____

_____

2. How does it look to you?

_____

_____

_____

_____

_____

3. What can be added?

_____

_____

_____

_____

_____

_____

4. What can be subtracted?

_____

_____

_____

_____

_____

_____

_____

Master Bathroom

Peace Scale

Maximum functionality   **Moderate functionality**   **Least functionality**

1. How does it feel to you?

_____

_____

_____

_____

_____

_____

2. How does it look to you?

_____

_____

_____

_____

_____

_____

3. What can be added?

_____

_____

_____

_____

_____

_____

4. What can be subtracted?

_____

_____

_____

_____

_____

_____

_____

Master Closet

Peace Scale

Maximum functionality   **Moderate functionality**   **Least functionality**

1. How does it feel to you?

_____

_____

_____

_____

_____

2. How does it look to you?

_____

_____

_____

_____

_____

3. What can be added?

_____

_____

_____

_____

_____

_____

4. What can be subtracted?

_____

_____

_____

_____

_____

_____

_____

Bedroom #2

Peace Scale

Maximum functionality   **Moderate functionality**   **Least functionality**

1. How does it feel to you?

_____

_____

_____

_____

_____

_____

2. How does it look to you?

_____

_____

_____

_____

_____

_____

3. What can be added?

_____

_____

_____

_____

_____

_____

4. What can be subtracted?

_____

_____

_____

_____

_____

_____

_____

Bathroom # 1

Peace Scale

Maximum functionality   **Moderate functionality**   **Least functionality**

1. How does it feel to you?

_____

_____

_____

_____

_____

2. How does it look to you?

_____

_____

_____

_____

_____

_____

3. What can be added?

_____

_____

_____

_____

_____

_____

4. What can be subtracted?

_____

_____

_____

_____

_____

_____

_____

Bathroom #2

Peace Scale

Maximum functionality   **Moderate functionality**   **Least functionality**

1. How does it feel to you?

_____

_____

_____

_____

_____

2. How does it look to you?

_____

_____

_____

_____

_____

3. What can be added?

_____

_____

_____

_____

_____

_____

4. What can be subtracted?

_____

_____

_____

_____

_____

_____

_____

Bathroom #3

Peace Scale

Maximum functionality   **Moderate functionality**   **Least functionality**

1. How does it feel to you?

_____

_____

_____

_____

_____

_____

2. How does it look to you?

_____

_____

_____

_____

_____

_____

3. What can be added?

_____

_____

_____

_____

_____

_____

_____

4. What can be subtracted?

_____

_____

_____

_____

_____

_____

_____

Bedroom #3

Peace Scale

Maximum functionality   **Moderate functionality**   **Least functionality**

1. How does it feel to you?

_____

_____

_____

_____

_____

2. How does it look to you?

_____

_____

_____

_____

_____

3. What can be added?

_____

_____

_____

_____

_____

_____

4. What can be subtracted?

_____

_____

_____

_____

_____

_____

_____

Bedroom #4

Peace Scale

Maximum functionality   **Moderate functionality**   **Least functionality**

1. How does it feel to you?

_____

_____

_____

_____

_____

2. How does it look to you?

_____

_____

_____

_____

_____

_____

3. What can be added?

_____

_____

_____

_____

_____

_____

4. What can be subtracted?

_____

_____

_____

_____

_____

_____

_____

Bedroom # 5

Peace Scale

Maximum functionality   **Moderate functionality**   **Least functionality**

1. How does it feel to you?

_____

_____

_____

_____

_____

2. How does it look to you?

_____

_____

_____

_____

_____

3. What can be added?

_____

_____

_____

_____

_____

_____

4. What can be subtracted?

_____

_____

_____

_____

_____

_____

_____

Office

Peace Scale

Maximum functionality   **Moderate functionality**   **Least functionality**

1. How does it feel to you?

_____

_____

_____

_____

_____

2. How does it look to you?

_____

_____

_____

_____

_____

3. What can be added?

_____

_____

_____

_____

_____

_____

4. What can be subtracted?

_____

_____

_____

_____

_____

_____

_____

Basement

Peace Scale

Maximum functionality   **Moderate functionality**   **Least functionality**

1. How does it feel to you?

_____

_____

_____

_____

_____

2. How does it look to you?

_____

_____

_____

_____

_____

_____

3. What can be added?

_____

_____

_____

_____

_____

_____

4. What can be subtracted?

_____

_____

_____

_____

_____

_____

_____

Patio #1

Peace Scale

Maximum functionality   **Moderate functionality**   **Least functionality**

1. How does it feel to you?

_____

_____

_____

_____

_____

2. How does it look to you?

_____

_____

_____

_____

_____

3. What can be added?

_____

_____

_____

_____

_____

_____

4. What can be subtracted?

_____

_____

_____

_____

_____

_____

_____

Patio #2

Peace Scale

Maximum functionality   **Moderate functionality**   **Least functionality**

1. How does it feel to you?

_____

_____

_____

_____

_____

2. How does it look to you?

_____

_____

_____

_____

_____

_____

3. What can be added?

_____

_____

_____

_____

_____

_____

4. What can be subtracted?

_____

_____

_____

_____

_____

_____

_____

Miscellaneous

_____

_____

_____

_____

_____

_____

_____

_____

"Home is not a place... it's a feeling."

—Cecelia Ahern

Start Your Peaceful Journey

On a Peaceful Note......

*Peace is kind. Peace is decluttering. Peace is advocating.
Peace is healthy. Peace is necessary. Peace is lit. Peace
is yours if you grab it and don't look back.*

Now that we've discussed my background and given you some ideas, let's get started on your peaceful journey. I'm so excited that you are doing this for yourself. Please, at this moment, pat yourself on the back and celebrate. I just love that you have taken the initiative to start living a peaceful life. You're going to be addicted just like me. Before we go any further, I need you to say this pledge to yourself or to someone that will hold you accountable. Place your right hand over your chest, please. I know it may be silly, but let's have some fun in the process. Repeat after me:

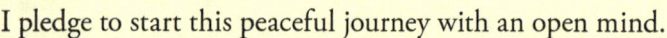

I pledge to start this peaceful journey with an open mind.
I pledge to be intentional.
I pledge to think before I act.
I pledge to always tend to my needs first.
I pledge to subtract people and things that no longer serve me.
I pledge to add people and things that bring me joy.
I pledge to let God lead me in this journey.

Now that you have said that pledge, let's get started on setting the tone for this journey ahead. The journey that I know you have been waiting on but needed a little assistance to get started.

Declutter

Sit down in your closest chair and look around your space. Do you see anything taking up space for no reason? If you do, get rid of it ASAP. We tend to over buy and clutter our homes and can barely maneuver around without bumping into something. That is borderline hoarding my friend. Go into every room and do this from top to bottom. I'm guilty of having pieces of clothing from high school that I probably won't ever wear again. It's so hard to let go because you think there will be some event you can wear it to later in life. Let it go. Let someone else wear it to an event. It has run its course in your home. Let go of items you don't use at least once a month. Pretty please. It is probably out of style anyway. You don't have to throw it away–you can give it to someone that's close to you, Goodwill, or a local shelter–but it's time to declutter.

Having too much in your space can cause anxiety and unnecessary stress. We always talk about decluttering our mind, but what about our space? Have you ever thought that one of the reasons you don't have the peace that you want is because you have fifteen similar red shirts or seventy Tupperware bowls without the matching lids? Let them go. I promise our God is a provider and he will supply you with a new set with matching lids. Now the longer you think about the items that you know you need to let go, the longer you'll have them. I know there is an excuse waiting on the tip of your tongue. Don't let the excuse get you; you get the excuse.

I was at my great aunt's house one day and we were going through her closet, and she had purses to last her two lifetimes. She brought out all the purses one by one and asked me what I thought. I told her my honest opinion of them. Some of the purses she had not worn in years. Some of the purses were out of style and just did not align with who she was at the time. Some were truly antiques and had to be kept. (I tried my best to get one from her, but she was not going for it at all.) She did not have a huge pile to give away, but she let some go. *She started somewhere.* That's all you have to do. I was looking at her like a proud mother on their child's first day of school. I'm so proud of you Aunt Virginia. Having a clearer space without too much but just enough is peace. Let it go friend. Doing this exercise will help you think clearer and help you to start your peaceful journey with all the extra space you'll need. Subtract the old and add the new items that you will incorporate into your new daily routine. Say it with me as you throw that shirt from 2007 away, "Out with the old and in with the new."

Now that you have cleared up some space for items that will go toward your new peaceful journey, rest a little while. Don't rest too long and please don't go digging in that pile to get stuff out. Yep, I know you and I haven't even met you. Now that you have cleared some space and can think clearly, think about your health.

Body Check-in

Think about how your body feels. Do you feel bloated, tired, or does your body hurt all the time? If you are experiencing any of those things, it is time to put that foot of yours down and do something about it if you haven't already. How can you live a peaceful life and you're not feeling well? YOU CAN'T. Yes, I screamed at you because I need to make sure it sticks with you.

Start making appointments to see your doctors today. What I am about to say next is so important that your life truly depends on it. In the process of meeting with doctors and explaining to them what is going on with YOUR body, you have to advocate. You are your biggest advocate. You can't just go in the doctor's office accepting any ole thing. Your doctors will advocate for you to a certain degree, but you are the driver of your life. Ask all the questions you need to ask.

Spend all the money necessary. Health is wealth, my friend. Don't do yourself a disservice because you don't want to spend $250 for that MRI that could give you the answers you are seeking. Trust me, that shopping spree can wait until another time.

> In the process of meeting with doctors and explaining to them what is going on with YOUR body, you have to advocate. You are your biggest advocate.

If the doctors are requesting that a certain test be run, do the test, pretty please. There is such a thing called a "payment plan." Get you one set up and keep it moving.

Finding the right doctors is also important to help you along this journey. It is ok to fire and hire new doctors. I have done it plenty of times. Get you a medical dream team. Get you a team that is willing to listen, run tests even if they are not recommending them, and respond on MyChart (or whatever portal they use) when you have concerns. A lot of times, doctors are counting our pockets when we ask to get a test they don't think needs to be done. In the most respectful way, just say, "I got it." Because when it comes to my health, I will have the money every time. And the same should be true for you.

While you are getting those doctors in place, also think about your daily health regimen. Vitamins are just as important as going to the doctor. Choose a brand that is worthy of purchasing. Get your D3, Vitamin C, turmeric, biotin, a one-a-day multivitamin, and magnesium just to name a few. Maintaining your vitamin levels are important for you to think clearly, for your organs to function properly, and to be ambulatory as long as you can. If you're thinking about the cost of it all, I totally get it. Things are very expensive and the way the economy is set up today a lot of us are working multiple jobs. Consider eliminating a few expensive things in order to shift some of your funds toward your health. And if you don't want to eliminate them all together, just cut back some. Think about how long you want to live and be healthy.

I love natural remedies. Go to the market or grocery store and get things such as ginger, turmeric, cayenne pepper, super greens, and lemons and make some daily wellness shots. I ordered shot glasses off of Amazon to keep from having to buy the ones in the grocery store every week. There are so many herbs and oils that have great medical benefits. I advise you to always do your research on each of them, though, or contact a natural doctor.

A lot of the time, we feel the way we feel because of what we eat and drink. Are you eating fast food every day? Are you eating/drinking a lot of sugar? A lot of fried foods? Not enough water? If you answered yes to any of those questions, then today is the day you start anew. Throw out all the unhealthy foods and drinks (or go ahead and eat it to not waste money). But replace those items with healthier ones. There is a plethora of options to consider. You just have to be willing to give them a try and be more intentional about what goes into your body. If you are tired of that stomach being upset, get food recommendations that will promote a healthier gut. If your kidneys are screaming friend (that was me), find ways to help you drink more water. Adding lemon or limes is a great way to get yourself to drink more water. Do what you have to do *today*. If your head is constantly hurting, then you may be eating a lot of salt. Cut back on the salt and use other seasonings. I'm no doctor at all, but these are things that have helped me along my journey.

It is vital that you do a body check-in at least once a week. Make the time to put you first and assess the way you are feeling. Please don't ignore the feelings. I'm not saying go broke or take up all your time to have great health; I am saying prioritize, friend.

Mental Health

Not only is your physical health important, but your mental health is important too. Remember that your mind helps you control your body and what it does. If your mental is not in a good space, your body will act accordingly. If you have been struggling with mental health issues due to past or present trauma, heal it. Don't allow your mind to lead you down a path of destruction. Seek all the professional help you can. Put your pride to the side *today* for a better *tomorrow*. Let me repeat that for you. Put your pride to the side *today* for a better tomorrow. I bet you're over there thinking about how putting someone else in your business is not something you want to do. Often times we go to our loved ones for advice about what we are going through, and a lot of the time they respond with "I will pray for you" or "Everything will be ok." They give you mostly surface level responses.

Everything will be ok once you start taking actions and healing from that trauma. That's what therapists were created for. Please use them. They are trained to utilize numerous techniques for different situations and help you get to the bottom of your issue. You not only want to be able to get to the bottom of issues, but you want to learn better coping mechanisms. You want to learn how to cope with life events because they will like likely be embedded in your brain forever. And most importantly, you don't want to pass that trauma down to your children if you have them or plan on having them.

When you are triggered, you want to have a HEALTHY way to cope in that moment. My first job out of graduate school was as a therapist, and it was amazing. The sessions were lit and rewarding for the client and myself. And when I say they were lit, I mean a ten-year-old client had me rapping Mike Jones with her. I had to become a rapper to build rapport with her and it worked. I'm not saying that all therapists will turn into rappers for you. Just let your therapist know what works for you and what does not. A therapist will ask questions to help you break stuff down from the beginning. As a therapist, I said things to clients that their families did not have the strength to say. I remember a session with a guy who often manipulated his ex-wife. They were in therapy learning how to move forward and co-parent in a healthy manner. I asked him questions like, "Who do you think you are? What gives you the right to manipulate someone? What if someone were to repeatedly manipulate you?" He was not ready for those questions. He probably hated me after that session. But guess what? He came back time after time.

Now just imagine: Your space is clearer, your body feels like you can run marathons, and your mind is free of distraction and trauma. Can't you already smell the peace creeping in the cracks of your door? Pause and take some deep breaths if you need to take them. Be intentional in this moment, please. Become aware of your body in this moment.

- How does your body truly feel?
- What is causing you the most trouble?
- What can you do about it?
- What's on your mind?
- What is causing you the most anxiety?
- What trauma is holding you back from letting down your guard?
- What is in your space that needs to go?
- What can be organized better?

Start here on your peace journey. How can one truly enjoy themselves if you are out in the world trying to date and all you can think about is if this person is going to do the same thing as the last person. How can you be active in a sports club or at the gym if you're in pain all the time? If your house is full of old crap and you have things that take up space in every corner, how are you getting around your own home? How are you entertaining guests without being embarrassed? HOW? Start with the advice in this chapter and thank me later.

"Set your peace of mind as your highest goal and organize your life around it."

—*Brian Tracy*

CHAPTER 8

Peace in the Bible

On a peaceful note......

*Peace is GOD. Peace is praise AND worship. Peace is
weeping at God's feet. Peace is steadfast. Peace is faithful.
Peace is worthy. Peace is obedience. Peace is eternity.*

Now I know you didn't think I was going to write this book and not mention our Lord and savior Jesus Christ. Well, I have mentioned him earlier, but it was brief. I must start off by just saying God is peace. Hold on let me say that again: *God is peace.* If you spend time with God and understand his words, you will truly know what peace feels like. I'm not a pastor, and I will never claim to be one unless God has that planned for me in the future. But I am going to let him use me in this chapter how he sees fit.

I had you get your favorite drinks and snacks in the beginning of this book. I even had you moving around to places that were peaceful to you. You have cleaned out rooms in your house, which I know you are thanking me for. You have even sat in a therapy session with me. But one thing you have yet to do with me is praise the Lord. Just pretend you're at church and its praise and worship time. If you grew up in a Baptist church, you'll really be able to follow me. Get up on your feet church and show God that you love and appreciate him.

Y'all not hearing me.

I said get up on your feet and show the almighty God that you love him and can't live without him. Put on your favorite gospel song and just jam for a second. Throw your hands up. Run back and forth if you need to. Just don't hurt yourself. I saw people get hurt and wigs flying during praise and worship as a young girl. I tried my best not to laugh during those times, but I just couldn't help myself. (God, please forgive me. I didn't know any better).

Think about what God has done in your life. Think about when you wanted to choose violence, but you chose peace instead. That was God. Ain't he good? All the time. Now that we have had our praise and worship, we can get started with the word, y'all. You can't start a good word without including praise and worship. Whew I'm fired up for the word today. I hope y'all ready.

Open your bible, so you can highlight the scriptures that discuss peace. You can also use this time to take notes, as you would in church. The scriptures we discuss will be interpreted in *my* understanding. Remember, I'm letting God use me how he sees fit. Alright y'all, let's get into the word.

> *"And the effect of righteousness will be peace, and the result of righteousness, quietness and trust forever. My people will abide in a peaceful habitation, in secure dwellings, and in quiet resting places."*
>
> *(Isaiah 32:117–18)*

We have to start there, because if you are out in the world doing right and abiding by God's word, that is instant peace. BOOM! *Drops mic and exists stage left.* God is saying that the results from someone who is staying in the word is a quiet and peaceful life. And within that is also his trust that he is going to always guide you in this life. Guide you down a path of peace that man cannot. Now let's get into this second part real quick. Wait for it... Your habitation will be peaceful. Who doesn't want the place they lay their head to be peaceful? That mansion of yours is going to be full of angels, trumpet players, and a table full of food and wine. Just imagine sitting next to angels. Now that is peace. Your home can be secure and quiet with God as the leader.

> *"Turn away from evil and do good; seek peace and pursue it."*
>
> *(Old Testament, Psalm 34:14)*

Right now, in 2025 with all the stressors around us, is the perfect time to turn away from evil ways. Anything that is evil, get away from it. Leave that evil mess behind you. Being part of anything that is evil is beneath you, friend. There is light in front of you and that is what God wants for you always. He created the concept of peace because that is what he wants for his people. Duh! He created a world for us to live in community with our brothers and sisters happily and PEACEFULLY! I rebuke you in the name of Jesus, Satan.

Once you expose yourself to God, continue to pursue him. Pursue him like your life depends on it. If you really think about it, your life truly does depend on it. You can't just stop at going to church one time or reading your daily devotions. It is much bigger than that. Read the entire bible. Take as long as you need to, but read the whole thing. Take notes on what you read; don't just read to be reading. *Read for understanding.* You will go through situations in life that will require you to go back to certain chapters for a reminder on how to handle that situation. Go to church and actually be part of that church. Most churches have small groups, weekly bible studies, conferences, and more. If you can't do them all, start off by doing one. You can open your laptop or phone and go to YouTube and watch virtual bible studies. And when you feel that you are 100 percent ready, take the next step and get baptized if you're not already. God loves you and wants you to pursue all of what he has to offer. And getting baptized just shows God that you are committed to him for the rest of your life no matter that happens. I want you to always remember that a life with God is a life worth living. Say this with me church, "God is good all the time, and all the time God is good."

> *"Behold, God is my salvation; I will trust, and will not*
> *be afraid; for the LORD GOD is my strength and my*
> *song, and he has become my salvation"*
>
> *(Isaiah 12:12)*

"This is why, for Christ's sake, I delight in weakness,
in insults, in hardships, in persecutions, in difficulties.
For when I am weak, then I am strong."
(2 Corinthians 12:9–10)

I hope y'all listening in here today, now. SHOUT if you're listening. (I put shout in capital letters because the preacher would say it loud.)

The Lord is my salvation and he is my strength. We are weak without the Lord. I was at a service at Victory Church in Atlanta on September 29, 2024. The pastor ate that sermon up. The pastor said we are very weak on our own, but with God we are strong. God is our warrior. God is why we got through that illness. God is why when you were depressed you got out that bed and sought some type of help. God is why when your manager made you mad and you wanted to knock everything off the desk, you decided to take a deep breath instead and walk on out. I don't think the people in that back pew are hearing me.

God is why you were pushed to make a 180 and change your life for the better, friend. Don't you dare sit there and take all the credit for your life and the way it has turned out. Friend, you play a part in it, but God was the force behind it all. Period. If we can do everything on our own, what do we need God for? I cannot, at the age of thirty-three, imagine a life without God, nor will I ever try to.

"For God is not a God of Confusion but of peace."
(1 Corinthians 14:33)

I remember when I was growing up my paternal grandfather would sit on the side of the church with the deacons every Sunday and hum the same hymns. He would hum it the same way every time and did it faithfully every Sunday. He never missed a day of Church until he got really sick. My siblings, cousins, and I would make fun of the hymns simply because we did not understand what or why he was hymning. We would say to each other, "Look at Grandad humming that same ole hymn." We knew it was church related of course, but we didn't know the actual words. What was the purpose behind hymning? We could have simply asked him, but we chose not to and laughed every Sunday instead. Don't judge me, y'all, I know it was childish, but hey, I was a child. I'm simply telling you this story because many times we will not understand something being preached to us or something that we are reading in the bible. Sometimes, we'll continue to not understand and form our own negative or confusing opinion. We'll laugh at it time after time.

My cousins and I were confused about the hymns, and you may be confused about God and his words. Don't be like us and not ask questions. Muster up the courage to obtain clarity, so that you can enjoy learning about the bible and everything that is has to offer. God does not bring confusion to his people but only brings peace and abundance. An abundance of knowledge, that is. It is easy for you to assume anything, but it can also be easy to do a google search and find a credible website that will elaborate on whatever it is that you don't understand.

It is taking me a while to read the entire bible because I am dissecting each chapter to understand it to the fullest. I want to understand for myself so that I can share and engage in conversations about the topic when it comes up. You can also go to your pastor, a church member, or family members to discuss the topic at hand. Trust me, you will thank yourself later for not assuming or thinking anything in the bible or church is confusing. Remember, anything attached to God is not meant to be confusing at all. When I hear hymns now, I am delighted because it gives me such nostalgia about my childhood in the church.

Whew! I feel like we're having a breakthrough up in here, church. Stand on your feet to get ready for a breakthrough in your life. I'm not the one to force God on someone, but I will always share his word and invite you to church. Now what you decide to do with the word is on you, friend. I'm just a child of God and it is a duty of mine to share the word with as many people as I can. If you know anything about Baptist church praise and worships, you must know this song, but if you don't I know your phone is sitting in your lap or somewhere close by. Search for the song "How Great Is Our God" and lift those hands up and praise. God has been great and has shown up time after time for you. While you're up praising the Lord look to your closest neighbor for this next verse.

> *"Finally, brothers, rejoice. Aim for restoration, comfort one another, agree with one another, live in peace; and the God of love and peace will be with you."*
> *(2 Corinthians 14:33)*

Let your neighbor know that you love them and chant how good God is and what he stands for. I'm sweating y'all. This is one of my favorite chapters. Give your neighbor a hug, handshake, or a look if you don't like touching. Reach out to someone that you have wronged or has wronged you and make it right or at least obtain some closure. Restore that relationship with whomever that person is. Forgive them for not showing up how you wish they would have many years ago. Once you do those things, you will start to feel much lighter and at peace. Get that baggage off of you. I'm in a season of healing, and it has not been the easiest thing to do at all. When I finally let my guard down and forgave my mother for things that happened to me as a young girl and for things she did not teach me, I felt a weight lifted off of my shoulders. It allowed me to be at peace with what happened and look past why it happened.

> *"Do not be anxious about anything, but in everything by prayer and supplication with thanksgiving let your requests be known to God. And the peace of God, which surpasses all understanding, will guard your hearts and your minds in Christ Jesus."*
>
> *(Philippians 4:6–7)*

You are probably sitting there right now reading this book and also anxious about something. Yep. I just called you out. What is it that has you anxious? Why are you anxious about it? How long have you been anxious about it? I just had to throw those questions out there. But I know you read that scripture before I asked those questions though.

Being anxious is normal; trust me, I get it. I have been anxious plenty of times about plenty of things. But the longer you are anxious about it, the longer you are not at peace, my friend. Go to your prayer room, closet, or wherever you pray the best, and pray about it. Pray it out. Pray until your mouth hurts, pray until dinner is ready, or pray until you fall asleep. Praying until you fall asleep is peace and you can't tell me otherwise. God is here for us always. He hears us even when we think he does not. He favors us. We are his favorites. He wants us to place our worries on his doorstep. You do know that God is the MOST almighty. God is the MOST high. God is the MOST amazing. Y'all got me preaching up in here today. I came to preach, but not preach preach. If you hear me, say "Amen." I need to know that you are awake.

"God will not put more on you than you can handle."
(1 Corinthians 10:13)

God said that not me. Whatever you are anxious about, you can get through it, because God gave it to you and, with prayer, he is going to help you get through it all. He gave it to you because he knows that you will find a way with him to get through it. You are one of his strongest soldiers. I wish y'all could see how hyped I was writing this chapter. I have had ups and downs for the past ten plus years because of the health issues that arose after having Lyme disease, but I prayed about it time after time. And I have gotten through it all, time after time. All the tests have come back negative, my mobility is still intact, I'm very active, and my mental is still in great shape. And most importantly, I'm *living* to fight another day. Yes, I got through it all, but it was because God was on the sideline running with me and whispering in my ears keep going. *Pray about it and don't be anxious.* I know you're still going to be anxious after praying about it, but let's meet in the middle. Don't be so anxious to the point where it is stealing all your peace.

"Now may the Lord of peace himself give you peace in
every way. The Lord be with you all."
(2 Thessalonians 5:23)

Now this is the one here. The Lord is peace. Everything that he shares is peace. His words are so wise and comforting. He offers the type of strength that man cannot. He is constantly reminding us that he is near. We cannot see him, but his presence is there. He is omnipotent. He said come to him with all of our worries. He is opening his arms to his children to offer love and guidance each and every day. Now that is something that we all should be sticking beside.

* * *

Now, take with you all that you have read in this chapter and practice it every day, friend. The Lord will give you peace in every way, just like the scripture said. Trust me, I know because my life is peaceful. I am peace. I spread peace. Let's pray and get ready to wrap it up.

Lord, I pray the person reading this book gives you a true chance. I pray that they can find what I have found in you. I pray that chaos leaves their life and for good. I pray that they realize they are a child of God and that when you made them, you wanted a peaceful life for them. I pray that they allow you to lead their life and welcome peace for eternity. I pray that this book helps them in some way gain the type of peace that they deserve. In Jesus's name, Amen!

"The more humble and obedient to God a man is, the more wise and at peace he will be in all that he does."
—Thomas à Kempis

CHAPTER 9

Peace Out

Whew. We made it to the end. As stated before, "I AM PROUD OF YOU FRIEND." It takes a lot of courage and accountability to realize when something is wrong and put forth the effort to correct it. You may not have known what peace was all these years. You may have grown up in a family of chaos since you were a young child and thought that was just how things were supposed to be. Chaos may be your middle name. You may have been afraid of change because of things you were afraid to lose. Let it go. I promise better will come.

I am in a stage of change, and it can be very uncomfortable. Trust me, I am experiencing it every day. Let me disclose what happened to me—maybe it will help you on your journey.

On July 1, 2024, I left a job that I had been at for almost three years. The job had its ups and downs just like most jobs. I loved it and was not planning on leaving at that time. But when new management arrived, it had more downs than ups. I was being mistreated due to taking FMLA (Family Medical Leave Act). I loved the role I was in and the money that I made. I went through all the proper channels to correct the situation, but none of it worked. So, I had to make a decision and fast. It was either stay in a toxic work environment and hope for change or leave and protect my peace. Guess what this girl did?

I put together a plan because I had to be smart about it. I had to make sure I was set when I left there. I applied for different jobs and got several offers, but God kept saying "Don't go to another full-time job right now." Whew! I was sweating bullets because the bills don't stop just because you stop working. Thank God for me having two jobs at the time. My second job was PRN, meaning it was on an as-needed basis. My manager at the second job offered to let me work there as much as I wanted, but there would be no benefits. Easy peasy, lemon squeezy; signed up for marketplace insurance, because where there's a will there's a way. Won't he do it. I just knew my peace was more important and I needed to respect myself and leave. Shortly after I got my marketplace insurance, your girl was gone.

I remember my last day so vividly. On the morning of July 1, I started packing my desk. I remember catching one of my coworkers watching me pack. She didn't say anything, but I think she knew what was going on. I just laughed to myself. I knew that was going to be my last day there. I was waiting on the HR specialist to email me so that we could meet. That previous week was hell, and we had to discuss what happened. The HR specialist was nice, but there was only so much she could do. HR is truly for the company in most situations. We sat in her office and talked for a while about the poor management (for the third or fourth time at that point). I was so stressed explaining to her everything that happened the previous week that my vision got very blurry. That is something that happens to me when I get super stressed.

I explained to her that that day was going to be my last and I had my two-weeks' notice typed up and ready to press send. She really tried to get me to stay and just take a leave. I wish y'all could have seen my face when she said that. "Take a leave only to come back to the same problems?" was my response. I asked her to cash me out and let me be on my way. I finished out that day just so I could tell some of my favorite people bye. They were sad and so was I. It was never my plan to retire from there, but I had one more year in me at least. When I arrived home that day, your girl felt so freeeeee. A burst of energy came upon me. I washed my hair with Beyonce's Cécred hair care and danced in the bathroom to some of my favorite songs. Beyonce's song "Freedom" was one of the songs I played. I was free.

A weight had been lifted off my shoulders. I could finally breath again. My motivation to work on my personal projects came back. Do you see how being in a place that God knows you don't belong can hold you back? I started back working on this book and got to chapter 9 within two months of leaving. Won't he do it? Yes, he will. If you know, you know. And here we are with the finished product. Let me just pat myself on the back, because I have been through it, but I advocated for myself every step of the way. Go Ashley. Go Ashley go.

I did not realize how much fight I had in me until that situation. That situation not only led me to being motivated again, but it also taught me to speak up, even if that means being the person that management no longer favors. When I am talking to family, friends, employers, and more, nothing in me wants to hold back now. I speak how I feel. I am respectful, but I am always going to tell the truth and advocate for myself. Period. I am at peace with who I am today and with my decisions. I am a strong educated Black woman that loves peace.

After reading my journey and following my tips, I hope and pray that you will learn to love peace too. Put you first for a change. Show the world what you are made of. Show the world what you were born to do. I was really born to be in the air (meaning, on someone's plane all the time). It's okay, though, it's coming slowly but surely. But back to you, friend. Be a leader and not a follower. Put your cape on and win those battles that are trying to steal your joy. Stand up tall and take what is yours. Open that door when peace comes knocking. Don't crack the door; open it wide and let it on in. Not only let it come in, but let it sit on the couch and drink some tea.

Sing it with me. "I love peace and peace loves me. I love peace and peace loves me. I love peace and peace loves me." Remember that song, so when that one coworker or friend tries you, just sing the song. Peace was made for you. It is yours for the taking. God created it for you to take advantage of. I pray that this book will be the catalyst to a peaceful life for you and those around you. I am a very social person, so pretty please speak to your girl if you see me out in the Atlanta streets. But for now, friend, I am sending you all the peace and love on this new journey of yours.

"Nothing can bring you peace but yourself."
—*Ralph Waldo Emerson*

Acknowledgments

God, I must start by saying thank you for bringing my parents together so that I could be possible. If it was not for you doing that, there would be no Ashley Chanae Green. Thank you for allowing my bigma to plant that seed in me when she did to get to know you better.

Although bigma is no longer with us, she played a huge part in my upbringing. She taught me lessons that will forever be close to my heart. She taught me how to cut tomatoes up real fine and be patient with cooking. She taught me that it is better to go slow so that you are putting love in your food. No one wants rushed food because it's most likely not going to be that great. She instilled in me the importance of family. Growing up, family was always around pouring into me. She is the reason why I prioritize spending time with my parents, siblings, and their beautiful children. Family will always be there no matter what. Through the ups and downs.

My family has always had my back, even when I did the most outrageous things. And for that I will forever be grateful for them. I could write an entire book about my family dynamics. I get emotional when I think of them sometimes. I love you guys to the moon and back. My parents have both been hard workers all of their lives, and so of course this girl adopted that trait. Thank you to my parents for instilling such an amazing work ethic. Thank you for showing me that you have to work to survive in this life. Thank you for supporting my dreams throughout the years, even if you were scared for me. Both of you allow me to live my life how I want to as long as it aligns with God's practices. Thank you for allowing me to leave home and experience life without the two of you in arms' reach. All of those things have helped me become the woman I am today.

I'm the youngest girl out of five children; I have two brothers and two sisters. God gave me a great batch of siblings. He really showed out on them. God, you always have done your big one in my life. I just couldn't imagine a life without you. Let's start from the oldest to the youngest. Crystal, thank you for always not only being a great big sister, but my second mother. You have showed up and showed out in so many ways. I truly owe the world to you. I mean that from the bottom of my little heart. You have taught me how to push forward despite the past. Watching you be a mother, sister, wife, and friend has instilled in me the power of juggling many hats. Jarvis, my favorite and only big brother we are similar in so many ways. We both tend to keep the peace and value history a lot. You have shown me that country living is amazing and worth it. If something goes down, we will survive because of the life skills that you have obtained. Ever since I was a little girl, you have protected me with everything in you. You taught me to be strong and fight through challenges. You have gotten into a few accidents that could have easily taken you up out of here. But with the grace of God and you being such a warrior, you are still standing. Thank you, bro, for never showing me what giving up looks like.

Melissa, hey girl hey. My twin that was born way before me. Thank you for always standing up for me and showing me what that looked like. When I was younger and the girls in my neighborhood bullied me, you were right there flying out the back door to face whoever it was. You did not play. I used to sit back and wish I was as brave as you are. Thank you for planting that seed in me to not take just any ole anything from anyone. You are my hero.

Joshua, my little knucklehead brother. Thank you for not telling on me when I did things I knew I was not supposed to do when we were kids. Thank you for showing me what it looks like to move forward when life constantly throws challenges your way. Love you big head.

Collectively all of you have been a huge part of who I am today. I thank you for pouring into me nonstop. Without you guys, I don't know if I would have thought to write a book.

And to my beautiful nieces and nephews, thank you for being you and preparing me for motherhood. I pray that this book will be motivation to you to write one someday or go after a dream you have. If TT Ashley can do it, so can you!

And to my readers, thank you for spending your hard-earned money to support me. Thank you for taking a chance to read my self-help book out of the million that are out there. It means the world to me friend. Until next time!

Wait! Not so fast. Thank you to two amazing, talented, fierce, and inspiring women that helped make this book a possibility. Monique Mensah and Sabrina Butler you two have truly outdone yourselves. I am so glad we crossed paths when we did. It was perfect timing. From hyping me up to telling me when something needed to be subtracted. You both have guided me and for that I am grateful. Until the next book ladies!

Dear Diary,

I woke up and chose peace...

Growing and Glowing Playlist

1. Carry-on by Akira Rae
2. Inner Vision by Valntna & ASMR Pink
3. Inner Me by Franchesca
4. i am so lucky by Sunshine Reigns
5. It's Already Mine by Shariya Wise
6. Self-Love by Londrelle
7. Gratitude by Londrelle
8. Peace and Love by Londrelle
9. Go Bravely by Londrelle
10. You Are Enough by Londrelle
11. Let the Trauma Go by Londrelle
12. A Beautiful Mess by Londrelle
13. Do it Anyway by Tasha Cobbs Leonard
14. I'm Getting Ready by Tasha Cobbs Leonard
15. If He did it Before... Same God by Tye Tribbett
16. Gracefully Broken by Tasha Cobbs Leonard
17. Depending on You by Gene Moore
18. I Need You Now by Smokie Norful
19. Break Every Chain by Tasha Cobbs Leonard
20. You Know My Name by Tasha Cobs Leonard
21. I Choose Peace by Yoneigh

Cozy Reads

1. *Women Who Heal: Natural Practices for Body and Soul* by Emma Drady
2. *We Should All Be Millionaires: A Woman's Guide to Earning More, Building Wealth, and Gaining Economic Power* by Rachel Rodgers
3. *Woman Evolve: Break Up with Your Fears and Revolutionize Your Life* by Sarah Jakes Roberts
4. *Don't Settle for Safe: Embracing the Uncomfortable to Become Unstoppable* by Sarah Jakes Roberts
5. *Pumpkin Spice Café* by Laurie Gilmore
6. *The Cinnamon Bun Book Store* by Laurie Gilmore
7. *Home Therapy* by Anita Yokota
8. *Self-Care for Black Women: 150 Ways to Radically Accept and Prioritize Your Mind, Body, and Soul* by Oludara Adeeyo
9. *The Four Agreements* by Don Miguel Ruiz
10. *Towards Rest: Discovering the Qualities of Rest for Our Lives of Faith* by Alabaster
11. The Good and Beautiful Bible study (volumes 1 and 2) by Alabaster
12. The Bible
13. *The Alchemist* by Paulo Coelho
14. *Summers Gift* by Jeniffer Ryan

Peaceful Places

1. Roswell Waterfalls
2. Amicalola Falls lodges and cabins
3. High Museum of Art
4. The Atlanta Beltline
5. Gibbs Garden
6. Helen, Ga
7. Stone Mountain
8. Hawaii
9. Punta Cana, Dominican Republican
10. Meiji Jingu in Japan
11. Chateau elan Spa
12. Victory Church
13. Vizcaya Museum and Gardens
14. Sharp Mountain Vineyards (Groupon)

Affirmations

1. I can find peace in many ways
2. Peace is showing up for me in the light and dark
3. Peace is cutting people off without explanations
4. I deserve peace in all things
5. I focus on solutions rather than problems
6. I am peace and peace is me
7. Sharing my peace is caring
8. My home is my sanctuary, and I treat it as such
9. I am a child of God, and he will forever bring me peace
10. When I put me first, I thrive
11. I cannot thrive in chaos, but only in calm
12. I am going to be all that I can be
13. I take care of myself mentally, physically, and emotionally
14. I take my lunch break no matter what
15. I get what I want out this life
16. I only get one life, so I will live like it
17. I wake up and choose peace
18. I deserve serenity in a world that won't let me rest
19. My body deserves good things
20. I can create peace from the smallest things

Ashley's Favorite Feel-Good Movies and Shows

1. *Notting Hill*
2. *Sleepless in Seattle*
3. *Matilda*
4. *Sweet Magnolias*
5. *With Love, Meghan*
6. *Family Reunion*
7. *Grey's Anatomy*
8. *Dream Home Makeover*
9. *Bridgerton*
10. *The Hughleys*
11. *The Princess and the Frog*
12. *My Wife & Kids*
13. *The Upshaws*

Mental Health Resources

1. *Retrain Your Brain: Cognitive Behavioral Therapy in 7 weeks: A Workbook for managing Depression and Anxiety* by Seth J. Gillihan PhD

2. *Healing Your Wounded Inner Child: A CBT Workbook to Overcome Past Trauma, Face Abandonment and Regain Emotional Stability* by Maria Clarke

3. *Don't Believe Everything You Think: Why Your Thinking is the Beginning & End of Suffering* by Joseph Nguyen

4. *The Body Keeps the Score: Brain, Mind, and Body in the Healing of Trauma* by Bessel van der Kolk M.D.

5. *How to Do the Work: Recognize Your Patterns, Heal from Your Past, and Create Your Self* by Dr. Nicole Lepera

6. *Self-Love Workbook for Women: Release Self-Doubt, Build Self-Compassion, and Embrace Who You Are* by Megan Logan MSW, LCSW

7. *Rewrite Your Life Story with Narrative Therapy: Change Way You See Yourself, Silence the Inner Critic, and Build a Life That Reflects Who You Truly Want to Be* by Vivienne Lennox

8. *Retelling the Stories of Our Lives: Everyday Narrative Therapy to Draw Inspiration and Transform Experience* by David Denborough

9. Psychologytoday.com

10. Betterhelp.com

11. Growtherapy.com

12. Headsupguys.com

Citations

Turner, F. J. (2017). *Social work treatment: Interlocking theoretical approaches* (6th ed.). OXFORD University Press.

Xi, J., & Lee, M. T. (2021). Inner peace as a contribution to human flourishing: a New Scale Developed from Ancient Wisdom. *Measuring Well-Being*, 435–481. https://doi.org/10.1093/oso/9780197512531.003.0016

www.ingramcontent.com/pod-product-compliance
Lightning Source LLC
Chambersburg PA
CBHW061757120626
46550CB00005B/2029

* 9 7 9 8 2 1 8 6 1 6 6 1 8 *